FROM COLLEGE TO CAREERS

FROM COLLEGE TO CAREERS
Listening in the Real World

ANGEL BISHOPPETTY

ROBERT ENGEL

HOUGHTON MIFFLIN COMPANY
Boston New York

Publisher: *Patricia A. Coryell*
Director of ESL Publishing: *Susan Maguire*
Senior Development Editor: *Kathleen Sands Boehmer*
Development Editor: *Donna Frankel*
Editorial Assistant: *Evangeline Bermas*
Senior Project Editor: *Margaret Park Bridges*
Senior Manufacturing Coordinator: *Renee Ostrowski*
Senior Marketing Manager: *Annamarie Rice*
Marketing Assistant: *Andrew Whitacre*

Cover images:
Clockwise from top left:
Doctor © by Rubberball Productions/Getty Images
Violinist © by Ryan McVay/Photodisc for Getty Images
Computer Scientist © by Thinkstock/Getty Images
Real Estate Agent © by Ryan McVay/Photodisc for Getty Images

Unit opening photographs: Unit 1: © by Chuck Savage/Corbis; Unit 2: © by Michael Newman /PhotoEdit; Unit 3: © by AP/Wide World Photos; Unit 4: Royalty-free by PhotoAlto/Getty Images; Unit 5: © by Michelle D. Bridwell /Getty Images; Unit 6: © by Michael Newman/Photo Edit.

For chapter notes, answer key, and other related instructor material, go to **http://college.hmco.com/esl/instructors**.
To obtain access to the Houghton Mifflin ESL instructor sites call 1-800-733-1717.
For additional student activities related to this book, go to **http://college.hmco.com/esl/students**.

Copyright© 2006 by Houghton Mifflin Company. All rights reserved.

No part of this work may be reproduced or transmitted in any form or by any means, electronic or mechanical, including photocopying and recording, or by any information storage or retrieval system without the prior written permission of Houghton Mifflin Company unless such copying is expressly permitted by federal copyright law. Address inquiries to College Permissions, Houghton Mifflin Company, 222 Berkeley Street, Boston, MA 02116-3764.

Printed in the U.S.A.

Library of Congress Control Number: 2005923829

ISBN: 0-618-38213-5

123456789-VHO-09 08 07 06 05

CONTENTS

Introduction xi

UNIT 1: COLLEGE LIFE 1
Skills Chart 1

1 Secrets to College Admissions 2
Prelistening 2
  Sharing Experiences 2
  Categorizing 4
Vocabulary 4
  Making Word Associations 4
  Filling in the Missing Words 5
Listening Comprehension Check 5
  Listening for Information 5
  Listening for Fillers 6
Discussion 7
  Sharing Experiences 7
  Think/Pair/Share 7
  Analyzing and Ranking Information 8
  Role-Playing 9
Further Study 10

2 A World of Ideas 11
Prelistening 11
  Sharing Ideas 11
Vocabulary 12
  Interviewing 12
  Matching 12
Listening Comprehension Check 13
  Listening for Details 13
  Making Inferences 13
  Listening for Missing Words 14
Discussion 14
  Expressing Opinions and Analyzing 14
Further Study 15

3 Sage on the Stage 16
Prelistening 16
  Agreeing or Disagreeing 16

Vocabulary 17
  Guessing Meaning from Context 17
  Identifying Definitions 18
Listening Comprehension Check 19
  Listening for Missing Words 19
  Listening for Descriptions and Definitions 20
  Note-Taking 20
Discussion 21
  Expressing Opinions and Ideas 21
  Making Inferences 21
Further Study 22

4 Do What You Love 23
Prelistening 23
  Think/Pair/Share 23
Vocabulary 24
  Guessing Meaning from Context 24
Listening Comprehension Check 24
  Listening for Information 24
  Choosing a Summary 25
Discussion 25
  Expressing Reasons 25
  Role-Playing 25
Further Study 27

5 When I Finish College, I Want to Be . . . 28
Prelistening 28
  Expressing Opinions and Persuading 28
Vocabulary 29
  Filling in the Missing Words 29
Listening Comprehension Check 29
  Listening Globally 29
  Listening for Details 30
Discussion 30
  Discussing Advantages and Disadvantages 30
  Giving Advice 31
  Twenty Questions 31
Further Study 32

UNIT 2: CAREER DECISIONS 33
Skills Chart 33

6 Rocket Science Smart 34
Prelistening 34
   Defending Choices and Drawing Conclusions 34
Vocabulary 35
   Using Grammatical Clues 35
   Categorizing 36
Listening Comprehension Check 36
   Listening for Chronological Sequence 36
   Listening for Information 37
   Listening for and Writing in the Past Tense 37
Discussion 37
   Sharing Ideas 37
Further Study 38

7 You Saved Me Fifty Bucks 39
Prelistening 39
   Expressing Opinions 39
Vocabulary 41
   Filling in the Missing Words 41
   Identifying Definitions 41
Listening Comprehension Check 42
   Listening for Information 42
   Listening for Expressions 43
Discussion 44
   Making Inferences and Expressing Opinions 44
   Negotiating 44
Further Study 45

8 I Just Knew It! 46
Prelistening 46
   Discussing Pros and Cons 46
   Sharing Experiences and Discussing a Quotation 47
Vocabulary 47
   Using Grammatical Clues 47
Listening Comprehension Check 48
   Listening for Cause and Effect 48
   Listening for Missing Words 49
Discussion 49
   Sharing Ideas 49
   Making Comparisons 50
Further Study 50

9 You Can Make a Difference 52
Prelistening 52
   Expressing Goals and Analyzing Quotations 52
Vocabulary 53
   Choosing the Meaning 53
   Matching 55
Listening Comprehension Check 55
   Listening for Specific Information 55
   Listening for Irregular Past Tense 57
Discussion 57
   Sharing Ideas 57
   Building Consensus 58
Further Study 58

10 I Fell in Love with the Natural Beauty 59
Prelistening 59
   Sharing Ideas 59
Vocabulary 60
   Interviewing 60
   Matching 60
Listening Comprehension Check 61
   Listening for Information 61
   Listening for Missing Words 62
Discussion 62
   Making Inferences 62
Further Study 64

11 They Pay Me for This 65
Prelistening 65
   Sharing Opinions 65
   Creating a Concept Map 66
Listening Comprehension Check 66
   Making Deductions 66
   Listening for Details 67
Discussion 67
   Supporting Opinions 67
   Interpreting Quotations 68
   The World's Funniest Joke 68
   Do and Make 69
Further Study 71

UNIT 3: DON'T JUDGE A BOOK BY ITS COVER 73
Skills Chart 73

12 Beauty Is in the Eye of the Beholder 74
Prelistening 74
   Think/Pair/Share 74
Vocabulary 75
   Interviewing 75
   Matching 76

Listening Comprehension Check 76
  Listening for Information 76
Discussion 77
  Expressing Ideas and Preferences 77
  Synthesizing Information 78
Further Study 79

13 Never Assume Anything 80
Prelistening 80
  Challenging Your Assumptions 80
  Categorizing 82
Vocabulary 82
  Guessing Meaning from Context 82
  Fill in the Missing Words 83
Listening Comprehension Check 83
  Listening for Information 83
  Listening for Minimal Encouragers 84
Discussion 84
  Sharing Ideas 84
  Think/Pair/Share 84
  Discussing Quotations 85
  Completing Quotations 85
Further Study 86

14 Computer Types 87
Prelistening 87
  Analyzing Stereotypes 87
  Completing a Statement 88
Vocabulary 89
  Matching 89
Listening Comprehension Check 89
  Listening for Missing Words 89
  Listening for Phrases 90
  Listening for Ideas 90
Discussion 90
  Expressing Opinions 90
Further Study 91

15 Why Cake and the Japanese Market Don't Mix 92
Prelistening 92
  Sharing Ideas 92
  Answering Questions 94
Vocabulary 95
  Matching 95
  Guessing Words 95
Listening Comprehension Check 95
  Listening for the Main Idea 95
  Listening for Information 96

Discussion 96
  Expressing Opinions and Making Inferences 96
Further Study 97

16 The Emerging Hispanic Market 98
Prelistening 98
  Expressing Opinions 98
Listening Comprehension Check 100
  Listening for Missing Words 100
  Listening for Details 100
Discussion 101
  Analyzing Ideas and Expressing Opinions 101
Further Study 101

UNIT 4: CROSS-CULTURAL MISCOMMUNICATION 103
Skills Chart 103

17 Everything Is NOT Okay 104
Prelistening 104
  Discussing Gestures 104
Vocabulary 106
  Filling in the Missing Words 106
Listening Comprehension Check 106
  Listening for Information and Making Inferences 106
  Choosing a Summary 107
Discussion 107
  Role-Playing and Discussing a Cultural Faux Pas 107
Further Study 108

18 The Spirit of African Hospitality 109
Prelistening 110
  Hypothesizing 110
  Africa Quiz 110
Vocabulary 111
  Matching 111
  Making Word Associations 111
Listening Comprehension Check 112
  Listening for Information 112
  Choosing a Summary 112
  Listening for Missing Words 113
Discussion 113
  Expressing Opinions 113
Further Study 114

19 It's Cool to Be Late 115
Prelistening 115
Discussing Cultural Time Concepts 115
Vocabulary 116
Making Word Associations 116
Listening Comprehension Check 117
Listening Globally 117
Listening for Information 117
Discussion 118
Making Comparisons 118
Discussing Assumptions 119
Phrasal Verbs 119
Further Study 120

20 What Part of NO Don't You Understand? 123
Prelistening 123
Analyzing Connotations 123
Vocabulary 124
Filling in the Missing Words 124
Listening Comprehension Check 125
Listening for Descriptions and Examples 125
Listening for Information 125
Discussion 126
Sharing Ideas 126
Further Study 126

21 It's All about the Contract 127
Prelistening 127
Sharing Cultural Perspectives 127
Vocabulary 128
Sharing Personal Information 128
Matching 128
Filling in the Missing Words 129
Listening Comprehension Check 129
Listening for Information 129
Listening for Ideas 130
Discussion 130
Analyzing Situations and Discussing Quotations 130
Using Expressions 131
Further Study 131

UNIT 5: CONTROVERSIAL TOPICS 133
Skills Chart 133

22 Happy Death 134
Prelistening 135
Creating a Concept Map 135
Vocabulary 135
Categorizing 135
Guessing Meaning from Context 136
Matching 137
Listening Comprehension Check 137
Listening for Definitions and Examples 137
Listening for Missing Words 138
Understanding Irony 138
Discussion 139
Discussing Pros and Cons 139
Scenarios: Expressing Opinions 139
Impromptu Speaking 140
Further Study 140

23 Prostitution in a Big City 142
Prelistening 142
Expressing Opinions 142
Think/Pair/Share 143
Vocabulary 143
Filling in the Missing Words 143
Listening Comprehension Check 144
Note-Taking 144
Summarizing 145
Discussion 145
Expressing Opinions 145
Analyzing Word Connotations 146
Further Study 148

24 Water Rights 149
Prelistening 149
Discussing a Literary Quotation 149
Vocabulary 150
Matching 150
Filling in the Missing Words 150

Listening Comprehension Check 151
  Listening for Ideas 151
  Listening for Information 151
Discussion 152
  Critical Thinking 152
  Maxims 153
Further Study 153

UNIT 6: MORE OF THE REAL WORLD 155

Unit Outline 155

A Texts, Lies, and Final Exams 156

Prelistening 156
  Sharing Ideas 156
Vocabulary 157
  Analyzing Word Families 157
  Guessing Meaning from Context 157
  Identifying Definitions 158
Listening Comprehension Check 158
  Note-Taking 158
  Listening for Details 159
Discussion 160
  Expressing Opinions and Analyzing Pros and Cons 160
Further Study 161

B I'd Always Wanted to... 162

Prelistening 162
  Sharing Expectations and Goals 162
Vocabulary 163
  Filling in the Missing Words 163
Listening Comprehension Check 164
  Listening for Chronological Sequence 164
  Listening for Details 164
  Listening for Past Tense 165
Discussion 165
  Expressing Opinions and Goals 165
  Impromptu Speaking 166
Further Study 166

C Permanent Materials Only 167

Prelistening 167
  Sharing Ideas 167
  Categorizing 168

Vocabulary 169
  Making Word Associations 169
Listening Comprehension Check 169
  Listening for Details 169
  Note-Taking 170
Discussion 170
  Sharing Ideas and Supporting Opinions 170
Further Study 171

D Doctors and Their Bedside Manners 172

Prelistening 172
  Supporting Opinions and Formulating Questions 172
Vocabulary 173
  Guessing Meaning from Context 173
  Filling in the Missing Words 174
  Using Homonyms 175
Listening Comprehension Check 176
  Listening for Information 176
Discussion 176
  Expressing Agreement or Disagreement 176
Further Study 178

E E Pluribus Unum 179

Prelistening 179
  Think/Pair/Share 179
Vocabulary 180
  Analyzing Word Families 180
Listening Comprehension Check 180
  Listening for Missing Words 180
  Note-Taking 182
Discussion 183
  Expressing Opinions 183
  Using If Clauses: Hypothetical or Possibility 183
Further Study 184

Appendix 187

INTRODUCTION

From College to Careers: Listening in the Real World is designed to expose high-intermediate to advanced level students to the challenges of unscripted, spontaneous speech. This innovative approach uses the authentic, natural language of native speakers, incorporates high-interest topics and amusing anecdotes, and prompts thought-provoking and cross-cultural discussion to help students bridge the gap from classroom language exposure to the challenges of comprehending native English speakers in the real world.

The speakers range from high school and college students to professors and physicians. In addition, they represent different regions of the United States and beyond, thereby exposing students to a variety of accents and speaking styles. The speakers talk about a wide variety of topics, including college admissions, diversity, approaches to teaching, career choices, marketing to other cultures, cross-cultural misunderstandings, cultural perceptions of time, business communication, euthanasia, and water rights, to name a few.

Why Authentic?

Over the years, we have observed many students who understand their teacher's English, but once they leave the classroom, they feel as though they are entering a different world. Subsequently, they become frustrated and discouraged when they cannot seem to understand anyone outside the classroom. Additionally, many of the listening materials used by teachers compound students' frustration because they consist of scripted recordings performed by professional actors. The students then wonder why the Americans they interact with never talk that way.

To compensate for the lack of authentic listening materials, we began recording people talking about their jobs and then created activities to accompany these audio segments. The initial recordings garnered positive responses from our colleagues and students, confirming our belief that there was a strong desire for this approach. Thus, we launched into this project.

Unique Features

Realizing that understanding a language is more than listening to audio segments, this text takes a holistic approach to developing listening comprehension. The text leads students through the process of activating background knowledge and experience, broadening academic vocabulary, developing and checking listening comprehension, and using interactive communication skills for discussion and critical thinking.

The centerpiece of this text is the real-world audio segments that contain various aspects of speech (e.g., pauses, fillers, false starts, repetition, corrections, varying speech rates) that are naturally delivered and include colorful expressions and idioms. Students have a rare opportunity to listen to a variety of accents, speech patterns, and reductions depending on the recorded speaker's home region, education, and age.

Also, teachers have greater flexibility. They can spend as much or as little time as they choose on each recording. They can focus primarily on listening strategies, or they can easily broaden the scope to develop a number of areas: vocabulary, interactive communication, presentation skills, critical thinking, research, and cultural awareness.

Organization

Each unit contains several chapters with a variety of activities and tasks. The activities in each chapter center on one authentic recording and consist of the following sections.

Prelistening

Prelistening starts with interactive activities that allow students to work with each other using their background knowledge and experience to share opinions and discuss topics related to the recording they will hear. Prelistening acts as a warm-up for the listening tasks.

Vocabulary

Vocabulary practice immediately follows the Prelistening and introduces key words, phrases, and expressions that students will hear in context in the recording. Many of the speakers are professors, so high-frequency academic vocabulary occurs repeatedly and naturally.

Listening Comprehension Checks

Listening Comprehension Checks are just that—opportunities for students to check how well they understand what they have heard. Most comprehension checks are divided into two or more parts, providing many occasions for students to focus on different types of listening, including main ideas, details, sequencing, and so on. The audio segments average two to three minutes in length, allowing enough time for the development of an idea without creating linguistic fatigue. The recording can be played two or more times as needed.

Discussion

The Discussion section leads students from discussing the content and ideas of the recordings to examining related current events and cultural perspectives and engaging in critical thinking and analysis. In addition, students complete a variety of tasks, including role-plays and surveys. Most discussion sections contain more ideas and activities than could normally be covered in the average class, which allows teachers to choose the activities that are appropriate for the makeup of their individual classes.

Further Study

Further Study contains several choices of tasks that students can pursue outside the classroom, either individually or in small groups. Many provide opportunities for students to interact with other students or with native speakers. In addition, there are writing and presentation projects so that students can apply the ideas and vocabulary explored in each chapter. Most of these exercises require some form of research (library or Internet) or some kind of data collection (interview someone, watch TV commercials, or report information). Many of the speaking assignments can be modified for writing assignments and vice versa, which allows for tailoring to the needs of the class.

Other Features

Other features of the text include Cultural Notes and Language Notes. These boxes provide additional information on interesting aspects of American culture and language and are found throughout the book.

Unit 6

The chapters in Unit 6, *More of the Real World*, may be used in lieu of or in addition to the ones in Units 1-5. Each chapter contains Listening Comprehension and Vocabulary practice that the teacher may choose to use as an assessment for each unit. The chapters also contain Prelistening Discussion, and Further Study activities.

To the Student

Have you ever said to your teacher, "I can understand you, but I can't understand people outside of class?" *From College to Careers: Listening in the Real World* is designed to help you make the transition from the classroom to the real world. By providing opportunities for you to listen to real language, the difficult aspects of natural speech will become easier to understand.

One thing to remember when listening in any environment is to focus on meaning as well as form. Don't let the challenging aspects of authentic speech distract you from your goal, which is understanding the speakers. For example, natural speech is not always grammatically correct—another reason that real-world language can be challenging. Use your knowledge of grammar, the topics, and your real-world experiences as starting points when trying to figure out what someone is saying but don't get stuck on the "correctness" of the language.

The recordings contain speech samples from a variety of people. You will listen to professors, students, doctors, computer scientists, businesspeople, and others discuss college, careers, and current event topics. You will need to listen to the recordings more than once. Each time you listen, you can use different listening strategies (e.g., listening for details, organization, main ideas). Besides developing your listening comprehension, you will expand your academic vocabulary, interactive communication, discussion, presentation, and research skills, and cultural awareness.

Another important feature of this book is the variety of cultural topics raised by the speakers. In addition to listening to speakers' real language, you will be exposed to American culture. The thought-provoking issues and cross-cultural topics are stimulating and provide an opportunity to participate actively in exchanges with your classmates.

We hope you enjoy the authenticity and spontaneity of the speakers as well as the chance for lively interaction with your classmates. Get ready to listen!

ACKNOWLEDGMENTS

We would like to express our thanks and appreciation to Susan Maguire, Director of ESL Programs at Houghton Mifflin, for recognizing our potential; to Kathy Sands-Boehmer from Houghton Mifflin and Donna Frankel from Bunker Hill Community College for their patience and editorial guidance. We also would like to thank our friends and colleagues who offered valuable suggestions: Jovita Acosta, Anne Andersen, Lydia Annayeva, Danielle Archinal, and Kim Dailey. The following reviewers contributed greatly to this text:

- Laurie Berry, Midlands Tech College
- Mary Diaz, Broward Community College
- Vicki Holmes, University of Nevada, Las Vegas
- Katie Hurter, North Harris College
- Kathleen Kelly, Passaic Community College
- Meredith Kemper, Florida Central Community College
- Marie Mitchell, Arizona State University
- Joseph Pettigrew, Boston University
- Gary Prostak, Los Angeles Mission College

We would like to thank all the members of the human race who regularly use language for communication. If we'd never had students, we would never have gotten this idea in the first place. So thanks all you language learners out there. Last but far from least, we'd like to thank our families who patiently put up with us 24/7.

From Robert:

Hiroko, thanks for putting up with my crazy hours. Max and Alex, thanks for your patience and for playing your video games quietly while I worked.

Mother, thanks for the inspiration you have provided with all the books you have written over the years. And to my late father: Thanks for always being there for me. You were the world's best editor, and your editing skills may actually have rubbed off on me just a little bit.

Thanks, Professor Bob Reid. Without the skills I learned from you in graduate school, this project would not have been possible.

Thanks also to the Bishop's/BishopPetty's for tea, snacks, and periodic meals.

From Angel:

Mom, thanks for your unwavering enthusiasm. Troy, thanks for supporting my dreams. Jade and Cora, thanks for understanding that Mommy is multifaceted. Dad, thanks for bringing home the fried chicken.

Hiroko, thanks for the great snacks and allowing me to take over the couch when Robert and I worked long hours.

COLLEGE LIFE

Skills Chart

Listening	Discussion/ Speaking	Vocabulary	Integrated Skills
■ Listening globally ■ Listening for • information • details • descriptions • definitions • missing words • fillers ■ Note-taking ■ Choosing a summary	■ Interviewing ■ Sharing ideas and experiences ■ Expressing opinions, reasons, and agreement ■ Persuading ■ Discussing advantages and disadvantages ■ Giving advice ■ Asking questions ■ Summarizing	■ Identifying definitions ■ Guessing meaning from context ■ Categorizing ■ Making word associations ■ Filling in the missing words	■ Building consensus ■ Making inferences and comparisons ■ Analyzing information ■ Role-playing ■ Hypothesizing ■ Creating a chart and timeline ■ Making a presentation ■ Writing an essay or paper

UNIT 1

CHAPTER 1
Secrets to College Admissions

Three incoming freshmen, Alex Schneiders, Stephanie Keens, and Megan McHugh, are talking about the college admissions process. These three high school classmates will be attending three different universities.

Chapter Objectives

- Sharing experiences
- Categorizing
- Making word associations
- Filling in the missing words
- Listening for information and fillers
- Building consensus
- Analyzing and ranking information
- Role-playing scenarios
- Conducting research for a presentation and making a presentation
- Hypothesizing
- Interviewing
- Making comparisons
- Writing an essay

Prelistening

Sharing Experiences

Discuss the following questions with a partner.

1. What types of courses did you take in high school? How much choice did you have in your schedule and course selection? How many elective

classes did you take? Did you try to avoid some courses? If so, which ones? Did you sign up for difficult courses to challenge yourself? Explain.

2. What is meant by *extracurricular activities*? How important do you think it is to participate in extracurricular activities? Why do you think some American universities, when choosing applicants for admission, consider extracurricular activities important?

3. Did you participate in extracurricular activities in high school? If so, which ones? Do you plan to participate in extracurricular activities in college? Why?

CULTURAL NOTE:

The SAT® and the ACT® are nationally standardized tests taken by millions of American high school juniors and seniors every year. The SAT® measures critical thinking, mathematical reasoning, and writing skills that students will need to succeed in college. The ACT® is more of a content-based test that measures English, mathematics, reading, and science skills necessary for college-level work. The ACT® also offers an optional writing test. A student's score on either test is usually one of several factors that universities consider in determining admissions. Frequently, students who receive a minimum score will automatically qualify for a university. The minimum score varies from college to college.

4. How important or useful do you think standardized tests such as the SAT or ACT are in evaluating a student's ability to succeed at a university?

Categorizing

Work with a partner to categorize the following terms. Then compare your choices with another pair of students in your class.

African-American Student Association	football	orchestra
animal shelter	Green Party	student newspaper
band	Hispanic Student Association	student radio station
choir	homeless center	tennis
College Republicans	League of Asian Students	wrestling
debate team	nursing home	Young Democrats

Communication	Politics	Ethnicity/Culture	Sports	Music	Service

Vocabulary

Making Word Associations

In each row, cross out the term that does not relate to the boldface word.

1. **athletics**	baseball	swimming	jogging	checkers
2. **atmosphere**	quiet	brave	noisy	quaint
3. **boost**	increase	damage	improve	enhance
4. **clubs**	art	Spanish	napping	poetry
5. **course**	music	English	biology	house
6. **diversity**	mostly men	all ages	various religions	different nationalities
7. **essay**	paper	composition	thesis	speech
8. **extracurriculars**	basketball	choir	lunch	tennis
9. **personality**	funny	thin	dynamic	boring
10. **organization**	cover	group	association	club

Filling in the Missing Words

Fill in the blanks with the most appropriate words.

admissions
apply for
fit in
getting into
heard of
make a judgment call

qualifying standard
scholarships
strength of schedule
thought processes
volunteer at

1. John and his wife _____ the homeless shelter once a week.
2. The race was very close, so the officials will have to _____.
3. _____ a good college was not easy for her.
4. He's a famous singer. I'm surprised that you've never _____ him.
5. Harvard has a very strict _____ policy. It's very hard to get accepted.
6. _____ refers to the level of difficulty of the courses that you take.
7. I can't imagine the _____ involved in creating a computer language.
8. He will _____ several _____ because his parents can't afford to send him to college.
9. The only _____ that the local college has is a minimum of a C average.
10. I joined the club, but everyone was so different from me that I just didn't _____.

Listening Comprehension Check

🎧 Listening for Information

Read the following questions. Then listen to the recording and circle the correct answer. More than one answer may be correct.

1. What are the most important factors that universities use to choose applicants for admission?
   a. grades
   b. quantity of courses
   c. strength of schedule
   d. types of courses

2. What does one of the speakers say about SAT scores?
   a. They are usually the only factor considered.
   b. They rarely make any difference.
   c. A high score will boost your chances for admission.
   d. Universities tend to use them as a qualifying standard.

3. What other factor(s) do universities consider for admission?
   a. extracurricular activities
   b. wealthy parents
   c. an interview
   d. students' career goals

4. Why is an essay important for admission?
   a. The admissions officers enjoy reading an essay.
   b. It is an opportunity for students who are not good test takers to show that they can communicate well.
   c. It helps the admissions officers determine whether the applicant will be a good fit for their university.
   d. Admissions officers want to be sure that students can think for themselves.

Listening for Fillers

Because of its spontaneity, informal speech produces a lot of meaningless or redundant words and sounds known as fillers (e.g., *um, er, uh, like, you know*). You will hear the speakers use several fillers. Look at the list. Then listen again and circle the fillers that you hear.

you know
whatever
well
I mean
like

Discussion

Sharing Experiences

Discuss the following.

1. Talk about your experiences applying for college admission. What do you feel made you stand out as a candidate? Talk about both your strengths and weaknesses.

2. What features, qualifications, or characteristics do you look for in a university?

CULTURAL NOTE:

A liberal arts college is a four-year institution of higher learning that is small in size and usually private. It offers a bachelor's degree and may have a limited number of graduate degrees. Students take a wide variety of liberal arts courses that focus on providing knowledge and intellectual enrichment (e.g., literature, music, history) instead of professional skills (e.g., medicine, law, business). Liberal arts courses generally serve as an entrée to professional or graduate schools, where students receive more specialized training.

Think / Pair / Share

Imagine that you are on the admissions committee for a small liberal arts college. Rank the following criteria for admissions in order of importance to you. Working in a small group (the other admissions committee members), discuss your choices and rank the criteria again. You must reach a consensus. Then compare your choices with another group.

essay	reputation of high school
ethnicity/race	SAT or ACT score
extracurricular activities	strength of schedule
grades/GPA	teacher recommendations
interview	top 10 percent of high school class
legacy (child of alumnus)	

Analyzing and Ranking Information

Read and discuss the profiles of the following four college applicants. Rank the students in order of first choice to last choice for admission to your Ivy League school. In a group (other members of the admissions committee), decide which applicant to admit.

	Pierre	**Juan**	**Pam**	**Suki**
Senior course schedule	• English • Literature • Geometry • Psychology • Astronomy • Creative Writing • Advanced Chinese	• English • Current Events • Basket Weaving • Golf • Home Economics • Philosophy	• International Business • Intermediate Spanish • Honors English • World Religions • Biology • Sociology	• Honors Math • Honors Science • Advanced Computer Science • History of Computers • Government • Business
Extracurricular activities	• Award-winning writer for school newspaper • Chinese club • Will be studying in a five-week Chinese-language immersion course in Beijing this summer	• Recruited by various colleges because he's a star player on the football and baseball teams	• Helps to build homes for the poor • Cares for dogs and cats at an animal shelter • Spent last summer in Latin America helping the homeless and practicing Spanish	• Chess club • Helps neighbors and friends with their computer problems • Updating her high school's computer system saved the school more than $50,000 this year
Grade Point Average (4.0 = all As)	3.72	3.4	3.65	3.8
Other	Ambitious; child of alumnus	Popular star athlete; the life of the party	Friendly, compassionate, and unselfish	Proud to be a "computer geek"

CULTURAL NOTE:

The Ivy League schools are a group of eight academically prestigious private universities in the northeastern United States: Brown University (Rhode Island), Columbia University (New York), Cornell University (New York), Dartmouth College (New Hampshire), Harvard University (Massachusetts), Princeton University (New Jersey), the University of Pennsylvania, and Yale University (Connecticut).

Role-Playing

Work with a classmate on one of the following admission interview scenarios. Take one of the roles and create a dialogue with your partner. After practicing, perform it for the class.

Scenario 1

Interviewer: You are reluctant to accept this applicant because of a low SAT score, but based on exceptional grades in high school, you think the applicant deserves an interview.

Applicant: You've never been a good standardized test taker, but you have an outstanding grade point average (GPA), have participated in a variety of extracurricular activities, and are very ambitious about your career.

Scenario 2

Interviewer: You are unsure about accepting someone who has a mediocre GPA, but you believe that because this applicant attended a reputable preparatory school, the applicant may have potential for your university.

Applicant: You want to emphasize that, despite your so-so grades, you have been attending an outstanding school with fierce competition, a demanding schedule, and time-consuming but worthwhile extracurricular activities. You plan to stress how well-rounded you are.

Scenario 3

Interviewer: You want this applicant to choose your university. This person has applied to a dozen top schools all over the country and has been accepted to all of them. You must persuasively talk about what makes your school special. Include information about your school's location, nearby attractions, and other appealing characteristics of your university.

Applicant: Though this school has a good reputation and the location is attractive, you're unsure whether the school or the city is the best fit for you. You need to get more information from the interviewer. Because you have been accepted to so many schools, you want to interview the recruiter about the university.

> **Scenario 4**

Interviewer: This applicant has a solid record and will probably do well at your university, yet the applicant appears to be a carbon copy of many others, and your university can accept only a limited number of students. You are not convinced that the student stands out in any way.

Applicant: You must sell the interviewer on what makes you unique (e.g., sports teams you were on, clubs you started, projects you did for classes, and short- and long-term goals).

Further Study

Choose from the following.

1. Many universities are referred to by their initials (e.g., NYU—New York University; U of I—University of Illinois or University of Iowa; UT—University of Texas or University of Tennessee). One speaker refers to USC, the school she will be attending. Look up USC on the Internet and find out which schools use these initials. Choose one of the USC schools and find information on admissions requirements, tuition, location, degrees offered, academic programs, school size, famous professors, extracurricular activities, and social life. Does it sound like a university you would like to attend? Why or why not? Present your findings to the class.

2. If you could attend a university anywhere in the world and you had unlimited money, which one would you choose? Research this school on the Internet. Prepare a presentation about the school and why you chose it. Report your findings to the class.

3. Ask three people what extracurricular activities they participated in when they were in high school or college. Ask them if they think extracurricular activities are an important part of college life and why. Report your findings to the class.

4. One of the speakers states that some universities require essays from applicants. She gives an example of a prompt: "Tell us a story about yourself." Write a five-paragraph essay using this prompt.

Web Activities

For additional activities related to this chapter, go to the *From College to Careers* website at **http://esl.college.hmco.com/students.**

CHAPTER 2
A World of Ideas

Gordon Gee is the chancellor of Vanderbilt University, a prestigious private university in Nashville, Tennessee. Dr. Gee previously served as the president of Brown University, The Ohio State University, the University of Colorado, and West Virginia University. He draws on this experience to share his view on diversity in education.

Chapter Objectives

- Sharing ideas
- Interviewing
- Identifying definitions
- Listening for details
- Making inferences
- Listening for missing words
- Expressing opinions and analyzing
- Agreeing or disagreeing
- Discussing pros and cons
- Conducting research for a paper/essay
- Writing a paper/essay
- Making comparisons
- Creating a chart and timeline

Prelistening

Sharing Ideas

Discuss the following questions with a partner.

1. What do you think it means to have a well-rounded education? Give specific examples.

2. How important do you think it is for students to have a variety of experiences before going to college? Explain your answer.

Vocabulary

Interviewing

Complete the chart by interviewing your classmates. Ask follow-up questions such as *What happened?*, *What kind?*, *When?*, *Where?* and *Why?* The boldface words are used by the speaker.

Find someone who has…	Name
been in a **band** or **orchestra**.	
been **involved in** an interesting project.	
traveled **extensively**.	
taken advantage of a special **opportunity**.	
lived in a large **community**.	
headed a club or organization.	

Matching

Match the terms on the left with their definitions on the right.

_____ 1. admitted   a. a woodwind instrument with a double reed

_____ 2. alike   b. a brief description of someone's life, work, and/or character

_____ 3. band major   c. accepted

_____ 4. bassoon   d. similar

_____ 5. broad   e. that is

_____ 6. i.e.   f. wide

_____ 7. profile   g. a person who leads a marching musical group

_____ 8. valedictorian   h. the top academic student in high school

Listening Comprehension Check

🎧 Listening for Details

Read the following questions or statements. Then listen to the recording and circle the correct answer. More than one answer may be correct.

1. According to the speaker, a college full of valedictorians would be uninteresting because they would _____ a lot alike.
   - a. look
   - b. think
   - c. learn
   - d. talk

2. What criteria are used for determining college admission?
   - a. geographic location
   - b. interview
   - c. background
   - d. interests
   - e. application submission date
   - f. essay

3. Which seven extracurricular activities does the speaker mention?
   - a. being a band major
   - b. playing bassoon in the orchestra
   - c. learning the banjo
   - d. starting a musical group
   - e. heading Junior Achievement
   - f. volunteering at an animal shelter
   - g. helping Habitat for Humanity
   - h. taking the opportunity to learn eight languages
   - i. playing on the football team
   - j. traveling extensively

🎧 Making Inferences

Review the following statements. Which of these statements do you think the speaker would agree with? Why?

   a. Variety in students' backgrounds makes a school more interesting and promotes more ideas.
   b. Students who are only academically smart make for an interesting school.
   c. Students who look, think, and talk alike are desirable.
   d. Extracurricular activities are more important than academics.
   e. Students should have a broad and engaging profile.

Listening for Missing Words

Listen again and fill in the missing words.

1. If we _____ admitted students by the numbers, i.e., by their grades or by their SAT, we would have a lot of valedictorians who probably would not, as a group, be a _____ interesting group of people....

2. So we really do take a look at the _____ person, or where they come from geographically, what their _____ has been, what interests they have.

3. The _____ of university, when everything is _____ down, the fact is that we're a world of ideas, and that's what we're about.

4. We want to make certain we have students with a _____ and _____ profile.

Discussion

Expressing Opinions and Analyzing

Discuss the following.

1. Refer to "Making Inferences" of the Listening Comprehension Check. Which of the statements do you agree with? Why?

2. The speaker mentions that if a university only admitted valedictorians, it would be an uninteresting place because the students would look, think, and talk alike. What do you think he means by this? Do you agree? Why or why not?

3. In the United States, diversity is often viewed as desirable. As the speaker noted, a university should include a student body with a diverse set of ideas. However, a diversity of ideas is only one type of diversity. Other types include ethnic, cultural, economic, religious, political, and geographical. In what ways is diversity important or unimportant? Explain.

4. Sometimes social change within a society comes from student movements or protests (e.g., peace demonstrations, civil rights movements, political protests). Is this a positive means of change? Why or why not? Explain which tactics used by students (e.g., hunger strikes, sit-ins, building takeovers, candlelight vigils, marches) are most likely to be effective. How can some of these tactics be harmful to their cause?

5. Many universities give minority students special consideration in admissions, a policy known as affirmative action. Some people believe that affirmative action encourages and allows those who have experienced societal disadvantages to attend an institution of higher learning. Others view affirmative action as a form of bias or reverse discrimination. Do you feel there are any instances in which minority students should be given advantages in admissions? Why or why not?

6. Some universities give preference in admissions to legacies, a term used for children of alumni. This legacy preference has recently been dropped by schools such as Texas A&M. Discuss the pros and cons of a school giving preference to the children of alumni. How does the practice help or harm the students? How does it impact the school?

Further Study

Choose from the following.

1. Gordon Gee is the chancellor of Vanderbilt University. Research and write a one-page paper on one of the following topics:
   - the duties and responsibilities of a chancellor
   - the history of Vanderbilt University or a university of your choice

2. Choose two universities. Research to compare the admissions criteria for undergraduate students of the two schools. Create a chart to illustrate your findings and present it to the class.

3. Think of the process you went through in preparing for and applying to an American university. Then create a timeline to illustrate this process. Here are some suggestions:
   - Started studying for the TOEFL
   - Took the TOEFL
   - Received your TOEFL score
   - Obtained the application form
   - Sent in your application
   - Got accepted to a university or an ESL program
   - Arrived in the United States
   - Started attending the university or ESL program

4. Admission preferences given to minority students have been challenged in the courts in recent years. Research *Hopewood v. Texas* (the University of Texas affirmative action case), *Gratz v. Bollinger* (the University of Michigan affirmative action case), or another court case challenging affirmative action. Then write an essay stating your opinion on the court's findings.

Web Activities

For additional activities related to this chapter, go to the *From College to Careers* website at **http://esl.college.hmco.com/students**.

CHAPTER 3

Sage on the Stage

Dr. Charles Miller, a professor of history, has written many articles and books on American environmental, cultural, and urban history and has served as the Centennial Lecturer for the U.S. Forest Service.

> **Chapter Objectives**
>
> - Agreeing or disagreeing
> - Guessing meaning from context
> - Identifying definitions
> - Listening for missing words
> - Listening for descriptions and definitions
> - Note-taking
> - Expressing opinions and ideas
> - Making inferences
> - Interviewing
> - Analyzing and synthesizing information
> - Making comparisons

Prelistening

Agreeing or Disagreeing

Discuss the following with a partner.

1. What do you think is the difference between a teacher-centered classroom and a student-centered classroom? Which one are you accustomed to? Explain.

2. Place a check mark next to each statement that a student-centered teacher would agree with. Then compare your choices with a classmate.

    _____ a. A teacher's knowledge should be challenged.

    _____ b. A teacher is the fount (source) of all knowledge.

    _____ c. Students should criticize teachers as much as teachers criticize students.

    _____ d. Teaching is a reciprocal process—the teacher and student learn from each other.

    _____ e. Knowledge can come only from the teacher.

    _____ f. The teacher should play the role of facilitator.

    _____ g. The teacher imparts knowledge by doing most of the talking.

    _____ h. The teacher's lecture should be an integral part of the class.

Vocabulary

Guessing Meaning from Context

Use a word from the following list to replace the underlined word(s) in each sentence.

analyzed   faculty   vessels
critical   retain   vision
debated

1. It's <u>important</u> that you contact Mr. Jones immediately.
2. The <u>containers</u> held a lot of water.
3. Even though Margie's boss has almost fired her many times, Margie has managed to <u>keep</u> her job.
4. The history department at my university has a large <u>staff</u>.
5. I don't agree with the president's <u>ideas</u> for the future.
6. After Robert and Chris <u>discussed the subject</u> for many hours, they came to an agreement.
7. The blood samples were <u>examined</u> in detail by the detective.

Identifying Definitions

Choose the answer that has a similar meaning.

1. abstract
    a. honest
    b. conceptual
    c. concrete

2. arrogant
    a. wanting to be attractive
    b. feeling of superiority
    c. lacking confidence

3. assumes
    a. plays a delicate instrument
    b. talks about differences
    c. accepts something to be true

4. conscious
    a. aware
    b. concerned
    c. puzzled

5. dialogue
    a. detour
    b. conversation
    c. building

6. discourse
    a. discussion
    b. discovery
    c. discount

7. exchange
    a. correction
    b. interaction
    c. devaluation

8. fundamentally
    a. basically
    b. interestingly
    c. jointly

9. intellectual
   a. indecent
   b. academic
   c. restful

10. one-on-one process
    a. a teacher working with one student
    b. a teacher teaching one subject at a time
    c. a teacher using one podium

11. reciprocal
    a. user-friendly
    b. hopeful
    c. mutually beneficial

12. rigorously
    a. slowly
    b. strongly
    c. finally

13. sage
    a. wise person
    b. lucky person
    c. young person

Listening Comprehension Check

Listening for Missing Words

Listen to the entire recording. Then listen again to the first half and fill in the missing words.

1. The faculty think that knowledge is something that is _____, debatable. And, therefore, the person who brings that knowledge in the case of the teacher is also _____ and challengeable.

2. If it's done properly, intellectual exchange, abstract thinking, political discourse, all of this stuff, is supposed to be _____. And that includes the person who bears the knowledge, most of all.

3. The European experience, as I understand it, and I've only seen it in action briefly so I don't want to extrapolate, but is usually perceived of as the professor as the fount of all _____, sage on the _____.

4. To use the sort of Socratic notion, "The unexamined life is not _____."

🎧 Listening for Descriptions and Definitions

Listen to the second half of the recording and answer the questions.

1. How does the speaker describe the experience of a senior student working on an honors thesis?
   _____
   _____

2. How does he describe the American way of learning?
   _____
   _____

3. How does he define the American vision of education?
   _____
   _____

🎧 Note-Taking

Listen to how the speaker compares the American style of teaching to those of other countries. Write the information under the appropriate headings in the table.

American	Other

Discussion

Expressing Opinions and Ideas

Discuss the following.

1. Dr. Miller compared the teaching styles of professors in American universities to those in European universities. Which teaching style do you think you would prefer? Why?
2. Do you think you would like to have Dr. Miller as a teacher? Why or why not?
3. What are your expectations from a professor? Do you think you would learn more from a teacher-centered or student-centered approach? Why?

Making Inferences

If you think Dr. Miller would agree with a statement, check **yes**. If you think Dr. Miller would not agree with a statement, check **no**. Listen to the recording again if necessary.

Yes	No	
_____	_____	1. Political discourse encourages abstract thinking.
_____	_____	2. Intellectual exchange in the classroom provides a wonderful learning environment for both professor and student.
_____	_____	3. By listening attentively to a lecture and taking notes, a student can easily retain the information for years.
_____	_____	4. Professors show their arrogance when they think that students are "just empty vessels that professors pour knowledge into."
_____	_____	5. A professor should assume that students are not knowledgeable enough in a particular subject to engage in critical dialogue.
_____	_____	6. Teaching should be a reciprocal process, whereby the students and professor study together.
_____	_____	7. If students don't agree with a professor's research methods, they have every right to criticize the professor so long as they can present a good argument.
_____	_____	8. Many issues are not clear-cut; therefore, students and even the professor can learn a lot from each other by debating these issues.

_____ _____ 9. Knowledge is meant to be debated.

_____ _____ 10. Since a professor is an expert, students should take everything the professor says as the truth.

Further Study

Choose from the following.

1. Interview a professor. Ask whether the professor agrees or disagrees with each of the ten statements in "Making Inferences". Then ask the professor to pick one of the statements and explain why he or she agrees or disagrees with it. Report the results of the survey and summarize the professor's explanation.

2. Ask a student and professor to explain the following:
   a. their expectations of a class
   b. their favorite teaching style
   c. their favorite type of teacher or student
   d. teacher-student relationships in and out of class

   Compare the results and report your findings to the class.

LANGUAGE NOTE:

In conversation, Americans generally use the words *college* and *university* interchangeably when referring to institutions of higher learning that offer four-year degree programs and award bachelor's degrees. In addition, a community or junior college is also often referred to as *college*. (I'm going to *college* in the fall.)

One instance in which Americans would not substitute *university* for *college* is when asking, "Where did you go to *college*?" (not Where did you go to *university*?) This question would be answered with the name of the university or college (e.g., Indiana University, the University of California at Northridge, Boston College).

Web Activities

For additional activities related to this chapter, go to the *From College to Careers* website at **http://esl.college.hmco.com/students**.

CHAPTER 4
Do What You Love

Victoria Aarons, a professor in the English department of a private university, recommends following your passion in choosing a career path. Dr. Aarons has written many books and essays in scholarly journals.

Chapter Objectives

- Building consensus
- Guessing meaning from context
- Listening for information
- Choosing a summary
- Expressing reasons
- Using persuasion in role-plays
- Interviewing
- Summarizing

Prelistening

Think / Pair / Share

1. List three professions that you think are the most prestigious. Then share your list with a partner. Do you agree with each other? If not, create a new list of the three most prestigious professions by combining your ideas with your partner's ideas. You must reach a consensus. Next compare your new list with another pair of students in your class.
2. Repeat the process by listing the three professions that you think are the most lucrative.
3. Repeat this process a third time by listing the three professions that you think are the least prestigious.
4. Plot the findings for the class. Create a graph that represents the professions for each of the three categories (most prestigious, most lucrative, and least prestigious) you discussed. Compare the graphs.

Vocabulary

Guessing Meaning from Context

Replace the underlined word(s) in each sentence.

advised	flying in the face of	set out
determined	initially	stick with
encourage	put off	typical

1. <u>At first</u>, I was overwhelmed by the amount of work required.
2. Even though my parents wanted me to study engineering, I decided to <u>continue in</u> the humanities.
3. My professor thought that I had ability as a writer, so she <u>counseled</u> me to continue my studies in English.
4. The <u>average</u> student starts college at the age of 18.
5. The homework assignment is confusing, so I'll <u>delay</u> doing it until I can get some clarification.
6. I <u>started</u> to go into medicine but changed my mind later.
7. She was offered a four-year scholarship in engineering, but she was <u>resolved</u> to study history.
8. Some students love English, so those are the students I try to <u>support</u>.
9. The student studied medicine instead of English to avoid <u>going against</u> her parents' wishes.

Listening Comprehension Check

🎧 *Listening for Information*

Listen to the recording and answer the questions.

1. According to the speaker, what do the students' parents want them to study?
   _____

2. How many students at this university set out to go into healthcare professions?
   _____

3. Why do these students choose careers in health sciences?
   _____

4. Which of the following courses does the speaker mention?
   - a. English
   - b. geography
   - c. history
   - d. organic chemistry
   - e. sociology

5. What reasons do the students give for putting off reading books for Dr. Aarons's classes?

Choosing a Summary

Listen again and choose the best summary.

a. Do what you love despite your parents' wishes.
b. Compromise your career choices to please your parents.
c. Study what you love because you'll do better at it.
d. Choose a career that you love only if your parents agree.

Discussion

Expressing Reasons

Discuss the following.

1. Why do you think that some students are encouraged by their parents to go into a healthcare profession?
2. What does Dr. Aarons mean when she states, "Those are the students I try to encourage without flying in the face of their parents' expectations of them"?
3. Why did you choose your major, or what do you plan to major in? What are your career goals?
4. Would your parents disapprove of certain career choices? If so, which ones and why? What would they consider a "real" career? Why?
5. Besides parental expectations, what factors influence career choice?

Role-Playing

At times, parents and their children may have disagreements about choosing career paths.

With a partner, study the chart and alternate between playing the role of a son or daughter and the role of a parent. As the son or daughter, try to persuade your father or mother that your career plan is the best choice for you. As a parent, tell your child your concerns about his or her career aspirations and try to persuade your child to follow your advice.

	Son/Daughter	**Parent**
Professional Basketball Player	You've set your sights on becoming a professional basketball player. You dream about a multimillion dollar salary, doing TV commercials, kids wearing your jersey number, and adoring fans chasing you. You believe that you can only achieve this dream if you "eat, sleep, and breathe basketball 24-7."	Many players try out for a few professional openings, and even if your son or daughter does make it, such careers are usually very short, especially if there is a major injury. You want your son or daughter to graduate from a university and study something that will lead to a career in case basketball doesn't work out. You need to encourage your son or daughter to have a backup plan and not put all his or her eggs in one basket.
Eastern Philosophy Professor	You've always been an academic type. You want to get a PhD in Eastern philosophy and become a professor so that you can read, research, teach, and constantly learn new things, making this a rewarding career.	It's a tremendous investment in time, energy, and money for an advanced degree that may not lead to a job. Even if your son or daughter is fortunate enough to get a job, it'll take many years to pay back school loans. You wish your child would be more practical and study Eastern philosophy in his or her spare time.
Soldier	You are deeply patriotic and want to serve your country. You've also dreamed of traveling around the world. You recently spoke to an Army recruiter and came away convinced that the military is the right career for you.	The military is a noble career, but you worry about the inherent dangers. And with all the moving around, it's not ideal for a stable family life. There are many other less dangerous ways to serve your country that are more conducive to a family life.
Stuntman/ Stuntwoman	You want constant excitement and challenge. Ever since you were a young child, you've been fascinated by stuntmen and stuntwomen in movies. And now you've decided that this is your calling. You plan to move to Hollywood to embark on this career.	You ask why your son or daughter intends to enter such a dangerous and unstable occupation when you can groom him or her to take over the family business. Taking over your company one day will also be exciting and challenging, just in a different way.

	Son/Daughter	**Parent**
Musician	Music is your life. In high school, you started your own band, and people were wild about your music. You want to do whatever it takes to become a star. You can't imagine doing anything else.	The music business is a crazy lifestyle. Not only is there no guarantee that your son or daughter will ever make it big, but the odds are that he or she will live on a shoestring budget for many years, if not forever. You are also concerned about exposure to drugs and alcohol. You wonder why your son or daughter can't get a real job and play music on weekends.

Further Study

Choose from the following.

1. With a partner, survey ten people and find out if they changed their career goals while attending college. Ask what major they started with, when they entered college, and what degree they eventually received. Report your findings to the class.

2. Interview three people to find out why they chose their fields. Summarize the interviews for the class.

3. The following are possible reasons for choosing a career. Add three more reasons to the list. Then ask five people to rank them in order of importance. Present the results to the class.
   - benefit to society
   - challenge
   - excitement or adventure
   - family pressure
   - good employment opportunities
   - personal satisfaction
   - prestige
   - salary

Web Activities

For additional activities related to this chapter, go to the *From College to Careers* website at **http://esl.college.hmco.com/students**.

CHAPTER 5

When I Finish College, I Want to Be . . .

In this segment, you will hear the same high school classmates you listened to in chapter 1 talk about their varied career plans.

Chapter Objectives

- Expressing opinions and persuading
- Filling in the missing words
- Listening globally
- Listening for details
- Discussing advantages and disadvantages
- Giving advice
- Asking questions
- Conducting research for a presentation or paper
- Gathering information
- Making a presentation
- Writing a paper

Prelistening

Expressing Opinions and Persuading

Working in small groups, discuss the advantages and disadvantages of a career in journalism, law, and nursing. Then decide which career is most appealing to you. Try to persuade others in your group that the career you chose is the most desirable.

Vocabulary

Filling in the Missing Words

Fill in the blanks with the most appropriate words.

area of
communicate with
communications degree
get involved in
hopefully

interacting with
passionate about
personal
see what happens
specialize

1. All his life he's wanted to _____ politics.
2. I don't know what the result will be. We'll have to _____.
3. When she becomes a law student, she plans to _____ in tax law.
4. He is _____ the environment. He just bought a hybrid car.
5. I want to get a(n) _____ so that I can become a famous broadcaster one day.
6. I'd rather not tell anyone else because it's _____.
7. Do you still _____ your ex-wife?
8. Plastic surgery is a(n) _____ medicine that I am not familiar with.
9. _____, it'll be a nice day for the graduation ceremony tomorrow.
10. He would be a better supervisor if he spent more time _____ his subordinates.

Listening Comprehension Check

Listening Globally

Listen to the three speakers. Then fill in the chart.

	Speaker 1	Speaker 2	Speaker 3
Goals			

Listening for Details

Listen to the recording and fill in the chart.

Definition	Term Used in Recording
complete high school or college (speaker 1)	
school for aspiring attorneys (speaker 2)	
four-year undergraduate degree (speaker 3)	
advanced degree that typically takes four to six years to complete (speaker 3)	
a nurse with many of the same duties, responsibilities, and skills as a physician (speaker 3)	

LANGUAGE NOTE:

Active duty refers to full-time service in the military. The *reserves* refers to part-time military service. However, reservists can be activated—called on to serve on active duty—at any time.

Discussion

Discussing Advantages and Disadvantages

Discuss the following.

1. The first speaker has already committed to the Navy for four years of active duty after college and four more years in the reserves. In the United States, many young people sign a contract to join the military after college; in exchange for their service, the government provides money for their education. What are the advantages of this approach for the individual and for society? What are the disadvantages?

2. What do you think the second speaker means by a "personal area of law"?

3. Why do you think the third speaker is considering taking a few years off between receiving her bachelor's degree and beginning a doctoral program?

4. Which of the speakers do you think is most likely to change her mind about her career? Why?

Giving Advice

Five specialties for each profession are listed in the chart. The three speakers want you to give them advice on what specialties they should each choose. With a partner, reach a consensus on your recommendation for each area. Compare your advice with another pair of students in your class.

Journalism	Law	Nursing
entertainment	divorce	geriatric
international	immigration	intensive care
investigative	international business	neonatal
political	personal injury	oncology
sports	tax	pediatric

Twenty Questions

Your class will be divided into two groups. One group will pick a profession from List A in the appendix (page 187). The other group may ask only yes or no questions until they can guess the correct occupation or until they have asked 20 questions. For example, the second group may ask questions like these:

- Is it dangerous? Is it stressful?
- Does it pay a lot? Is it prestigious?
- Does it mostly use your mental skills?
- Do you interact with a lot of people?

Then switch roles by having the first group ask questions about the professions in List B. Keep score if you like.

Further Study

Choose from the following.

1. Choose one of the careers that the speakers are interested in pursuing (i.e., journalism, law, or nursing). Then research and prepare a presentation on this field. Include information such as educational requirements, salary, work conditions, and responsibilities.

2. Research and write about the duties of a nurse practitioner or a physician's assistant. Then write why you think that this profession is becoming more common in the United States but is still uncommon in many other countries.

3. The first speaker mentions that she will have to serve in the Navy. Choose one of the following:
   a. Visit one of the military recruiting websites to obtain information on ROTC scholarships. Report your findings to the class.
   b. Visit one of the military recruiting websites to obtain information on the Montgomery GI Bill. Report your findings to the class.
   c. Call or visit a military recruiter and ask if noncitizens can join and what, if any, restrictions apply. Report your findings to the class.

Web Activities

For additional activities related to this chapter, go to the *From College to Careers* website at **http://esl.college.hmco.com/students.**

CAREER DECISIONS

Skills Chart

Listening	Speaking	Vocabulary	Integrated Skills
■ Listening for • specific information • cause and effect • details • missing words • chronological sequence • past tense • expressions	■ Interviewing ■ Sharing ideas and experiences ■ Discussing and interpreting quotations ■ Expressing opinions, preferences, goals, and agreement ■ Telling a joke ■ Discussing advantages and disadvantages ■ Supporting opinions ■ Negotiating ■ Describing a person	■ Identifying definitions ■ Categorizing ■ Choosing the meaning ■ Using grammatical clues ■ Filling in the missing words ■ Using *do* and *make*	■ Building consensus ■ Drawing conclusions ■ Analyzing data and quotations ■ Making inferences, comparisons, and deductions ■ Presenting a biographical sketch ■ Writing a critique or a paper ■ Creating a brochure and a concept map ■ Making a presentation

CHAPTER 6
Rocket Science Smart

Listen to Kimberly Bradley and the nontraditional way in which she became a physician. Also listen for Dr. Bradley's two medical specialties.

Chapter Objectives

- Defending choices and drawing conclusions
- Using grammatical clues
- Categorizing
- Listening for chronological sequence
- Listening for information
- Listening for and writing in the past tense
- Sharing ideas
- Describing a person
- Discussing advantages and disadvantages
- Conducting research for a presentation or paper
- Making a presentation
- Writing a paper

Prelistening

Defending Choices and Drawing Conclusions

Discuss the following with a partner.

1. Which one of these is most important to professional success: education, experience, or talent? Select one and be prepared to defend your choice. You may want to discuss with a partner what each term means before choosing the most important one.

2. The average American over the course of a lifetime changes jobs ten times and careers three times. What insights does this give you about American views of jobs, career, and education?

Vocabulary

Using Grammatical Clues

Use grammatical clues to match the first half of the sentence on the left with the second half of the sentence on the right. The underlined words are used by the speaker.

_____ 1. I was looking for career
_____ 2. Uncle Sam provided a
_____ 3. I <u>thoroughly</u> enjoyed my first
_____ 4. I decided to
_____ 5. Studying math wasn't as
_____ 6. One of my <u>part-time</u>
_____ 7. Ward rounds <u>consist of</u>
_____ 8. Working in the
_____ 9. While working in the hospital,
_____ 10. What I <u>discovered</u> was that these people were not smarter
_____ 11. They would <u>frequently</u> come
_____ 12. I would <u>jokingly</u> tell them that if
_____ 13. That <u>discovery</u> opened some <u>new horizons</u>

a. very nice <u>route</u> to college.
b. <u>interesting</u> as I thought it should be.
c. drawing blood on the patients in the hospital each morning.
d. hospital allowed me the opportunity to work with the residents and interns.
e. than me.
f. you <u>split</u> your <u>salary</u> with me, I'll tell you what that means.
g. for me.
h. <u>options</u>.
i. tour of duty.
j. <u>get out</u> of the Air Force when my first child was born.
k. jobs was working in the hospital lab.
l. I made a <u>fantastic discovery</u>.
m. to me with their questions.

Categorizing

Practice categorizing vocabulary by following these steps:

- Write the terms under the category headings in the chart. You may use a term more than once.
- Discuss your choices with a partner.
- Listen for how the terms are used in the recording.
- Reconsider how you categorized the words and make any necessary changes.

active duty	interns	residents
basic training	lab	tour of duty
enlisted	manipulation	Uncle Sam
graduate	medical technology	

Education	Medicine	Military

Listening Comprehension Check

Listening for Chronological Sequence

The speaker did many things between high school graduation and the beginning of medical school. Listen to the recording and number the events in chronological order. The first one has been done for you.

_____ studied medical technology in college

_____ had two children

_____ worked as a lab technician in the military

_____ studied math in college

____1___ enlisted in Air Force

_____ worked part-time doing ward rounds

🎧 Listening for Information

Listen to the recording and answer the questions.

1. What are Dr. Bradley's medical specialties?

   _____
   _____

2. Why did she delay attending college?

   _____
   _____

3. Why did she change her major in college?

   _____
   _____

4. What "fantastic discovery" did she make?

   _____
   _____

🎧 Listening for and Writing in the Past Tense

Practice the past tense by using the following steps:

- Listen again and write down the past tense verbs you hear.
- Compare your list to that of your partner and add any verbs you missed.
- Share your list with another pair of students. Add words you and your partner overlooked.
- Write a paragraph using past tense narration to tell a story about your education or career path or that of a family member or friend.

Discussion

Sharing Ideas

Discuss the following.

1. What did the speaker mean by rocket science smart? Do you know anyone who is rocket science smart? Describe that person.

2. The speaker refers to Uncle Sam. Who do you think he is? What role does he play in her life?

3. Many young people in the United States work for a few years between college and graduate school, but most students who attend medical school don't take any time off to work between college and medical school. Which do you think is preferable? Why?

4. It's not unusual for American college students to change their majors. What are the advantages and disadvantages of changing your major in the middle of your studies? Is this a common practice in other countries? Why or why not?

Further Study

Choose from the following.

1. Research the origin of Uncle Sam. Find out what this icon of American culture represents. Write a brief report on what you learned.

2. Research the history, training, and responsibilities of a flight surgeon, an osteopath, or another specialist. Include any unique aspects of the specialty. Present your findings to the class.

Web Activities

For additional activities related to this chapter, go to the *From College to Careers* website at **http://esl.college.hmco.com/students.**

CHAPTER 7
You Saved Me Fifty Bucks

Let's continue listening to Dr. Bradley.

Chapter Objectives

- Agreeing or disagreeing with a quote
- Expressing opinions
- Filling in the missing words
- Identifying definitions
- Listening for information and expressions
- Making inferences
- Expressing opinions
- Negotiating
- Conducting research for a presentation
- Interviewing
- Analyzing data
- Drawing conclusions
- Making a presentation

Prelistening

Expressing Opinions

Discuss the following with a partner.

1. *Wives and moms just don't make good medical students.* Do you agree with this statement? Why or why not? When you listen to the recording, notice how the speaker reacts to this comment.

2. Place a check mark by the occupations that you think are more suitable for men, those that are more suitable for women, and those that both men and women are equally suited for. Feel free to add any occupations. Then discuss your responses in small groups. As a class, tally the data and discuss the results.

Occupations	Men	Women	Both
astronaut			
business owner			
chef			
doctor			
engineer			
firefighter			
lawyer			
nurse			
president or prime minister			
secretary			
soldier			
sports reporter			
teacher			

Vocabulary

Filling in the Missing Words

Fill in the blanks with the most appropriate words.

application   major
exclusion   program
impressed with   relate to

1. Ahmed's _____ in college was engineering. His school has a well-known engineering _____.
2. Juanita was so _____ the courses offered that she submitted a(n) _____ to the University of Colorado.
3. Professor Franks spends almost all his time on research to the _____ of everything else, including his family. As a result, he sometimes cannot _____ his students.

Identifying Definitions

Choose the answer that has a similar meaning. More than one may be correct. The words are listed in the order the speaker uses them.

1. biology
   a. natural science
   b. physical science
   c. social science

2. arrogant
   a. full of pride
   b. warm and caring
   c. full of excitement

3. odd
   a. strange
   b. weird
   c. normal

4. attitude
   a. knowledge
   b. career goal
   c. way of thinking

5. selection
    a. thought
    b. choice
    c. pick

6. dedicate
    a. harm
    b. commit
    c. complicate

7. entire
    a. whole
    b. total
    c. incomplete

8. train (verb)
    a. move
    b. teach
    c. travel

9. general
    a. broad
    b. specific
    c. private

10. masses
    a. substances
    b. crowds
    c. drinks

Listening Comprehension Check

 Listening for Information

Listen to the recording and answer the following questions.

1. What school was Dr. Bradley first interested in attending?

2. How old was she when she enrolled in med school?

3. At what age did she get married?

4. What advice did the first interviewer give her? Did she follow his advice?

5. What other school was she interested in?

6. Why did the interviewer consider her arrogant?

7. Why did she consider TCOM (Texas College of Osteopathic Medicine) to be a good school?

LANGUAGE NOTE:

In casual conversation, shortened forms of words are common. The speaker uses the terms *med school* and *med tech training*. In these examples, *med* is short for medical, and *tech* is short for technical.

Listening for Expressions

Listen again and write three expressions the speaker uses that include the word *time*. Then guess the meaning of each expression.

Expression	Meaning

Discussion

Making Inferences and Expressing Opinions

Discuss the following.

1. What does Dr. Bradley imply when she says, "He saved me fifty bucks"? How do you think she reacted? How would you have reacted?

2. What do you think Dr. Bradley means when she says that doctors can't relate to their patients? Do you agree or disagree? Explain.

3. The attitude of the medical school official reflects the feelings of some that a woman should choose between motherhood and a career. Do you agree? Why or why not? In what way does this also apply to fatherhood? Is it possible to manage school, home, and career? If so, how?

Negotiating

You are serving as the admissions screener for your medical school. Rank each of the following four candidates in order from first to last choice for admission. Then make your recommendations to the rest of the admissions panel and negotiate for the one applicant you will admit.

Candidate A

This candidate maintained a 3.9 grade point average (GPA) at a state college. Following graduation, he was an archaeologist in Greece for two years before working in the Peace Corps in Africa for three years. His experience in Africa got him interested in health care, and he subsequently served as the executive director of a nonprofit health awareness organization.

Candidate B

This candidate obtained a 3.6 GPA at an Ivy League school. As a freshman, he had problems adjusting to college life and living away from home; thus, his grades suffered. However, his grades improved dramatically beginning in his sophomore year, due in large part to his ambition to attend medical school.

Candidate C

This candidate's GPA was 3.8 at the small liberal arts school she attended. Her college has a reputation for producing world-class physicians. The candidate has wanted to become a doctor since she was a toddler. She started reading medical journals in elementary school.

Candidate D

This candidate graduated from a large state university with a 3.75 GPA. Her father is a renowned heart surgeon; her mother, a respected pediatrician; and her brother, a well-known ophthalmologist. Her desire is to follow in her family's footsteps.

Further Study

Choose from the following.

1. Choose a medical school and research the specific qualifications for admission to that school. Present your findings to the class.

2. Ask someone for tips on balancing career, home, and family. Report the information to the class.

3. Complete the following steps.
   a. Survey five or more people. Ask them to name the types of medical specialists they have seen (general practitioner, urologist, optometrist, dentist, etc.).
   b. Find out the gender (male/female) of each practitioner.
   c. Record the information in the chart.
   d. Combine your data with others in your class.
   e. Analyze the data. What trends do you see? What are the implications of your results? Are gender and specialty correlated? Are doctors in some specialties more or less likely to be women or men? Do you think your results reflect the population at large? Present your analysis to the class.

Type of Practitioner/Specialist	Male or Female

Web Activities

For additional activities related to this chapter, go to the *From College to Careers* website at **http://esl.college.hmco.com/students**.

CHAPTER 8

I Just Knew It!

After listening to Dr. Stacey Bean, who practices internal medicine, be ready to compare her experiences with Dr. Bradley's experiences.

> **Chapter Objectives**
>
> - Discussing pros and cons
> - Sharing experiences and discussing a quotation
> - Using grammatical clues
> - Listening for cause and effect
> - Listening for missing words
> - Sharing ideas
> - Making comparisons
> - Conducting research for a paper/presentation
> - Making a presentation
> - Writing a paper

Prelistening

Discussing Pros and Cons

In a small group, discuss the advantages and disadvantages of being a doctor. Then discuss the advantages and disadvantages of being a teacher. Write the pros and cons in the chart.

Doctor		Teacher	
Pros	**Cons**	**Pros**	**Cons**

Sharing Experiences and Discussing a Quotation

Discuss the following questions.

1. Have you had a life-changing event (e.g., major illness or injury, wedding, birth of a sibling, birth of a child, inheritance)? Describe the event and how it affected you. Did it have an impact on your career choice? How?

2. *When fate hands you a lemon, make lemonade*—Dale Carnegie.
   What do you think this quotation means? Many Americans admire this approach to life. What does this imply about American culture?

Vocabulary

Using Grammatical Clues

Use grammatical clues to match the first half of the sentence on the left with the second half of the sentence on the right. The target phrases are underlined.

_____ 1. I <u>worked my tail off</u>

_____ 2. <u>To make a long story short</u>, the doctors discovered

_____ 3. I got behind

_____ 4. When dealing with

_____ 5. I couldn't eat any solid foods after getting

_____ 6. After changing careers,

a. that I had a rare disease.

b. with my work and had to play <u>catch-up</u>.

c. to make more money.

d. my <u>wisdom teeth pulled</u>.

e. my life felt <u>out of whack</u>.

f. the federal government, you have to go through <u>a lot of red tape</u>.

Listening Comprehension Check

Listening for Cause and Effect

Listen to the recording and answer the questions.

1. Which reasons did the speaker give for deciding against becoming a biology teacher?
   _____

2. Number the items to show the sequence of events in the speaker's life. With a partner, discuss the cause and effect relationships of each.

   _____ diagnosed with Gaucher's disease

   _____ affected by the kids at the Ronald McDonald House

   _____ had wisdom teeth removed

   _____ decided to become a doctor

   _____ participated in an NIH study

CULTURAL NOTE:

Gaucher's disease is a genetically inherited, enzyme-deficiency disorder. Symptoms may include anemia, fatigue, easy bruising, and a tendency to bleed. Although rare in the general population, this disease affects 1 in 850 Ashkenazi Jews (Jews of eastern European or German descent).

LANGUAGE NOTE:

The speaker refers to two government agencies: the FDA and the NIH. The FDA stands for the Food and Drug Administration, which is responsible for regulating food and medical treatments in the United States. The NIH, or the National Institutes of Health, conducts medical research.

Listening for Missing Words

Listen again and fill in the blanks.

But, anyhow, so I have Gaucher's disease, and it was a disease that was being studied (1) _____, at that time, at the National Institutes of Health in Bethesda, Maryland. So, off I go to college, and in December of my (2) _____ year in college, I go—I was accepted to this drug study in Maryland, I was in college in Georgia. And I was 18, and I got (3) _____ in the study and I started flying to Maryland, actually through Washington National Airport every two weeks for—well I'm still getting the medication. I was on the drug (4) _____ and actually it got (5) _____ by the FDA, and so, I'm still on it. But that (6) _____, being a patient at the NIH, and staying in the basically the (7) _____ of the Ronald McDonald House with the other kids there, just (8) _____ my life forever, and I knew that I had to be a doctor. I just knew it.

Discussion

Sharing Ideas

Discuss the following.

1. Discuss the reasons that the speaker mentions for not becoming a biology teacher. Did you list these reasons as pros or cons in the prelistening exercise? Did any of these reasons surprise you? If so, which one(s) and why?

2. The speaker said that she knew she had to be a doctor because of her experiences as a teenager. How did you choose your career?

3. Is it important for you to follow the same career path as your father or mother? Why or why not? Would your parents like you to follow in their footsteps? Why or why not?

4. The speaker participated in a drug study. How are these types of drug experiments beneficial or harmful? Would you participate in a drug study if you had an unusual health condition? Why or why not?

5. Refer to the quotation in the prelistening exercise. How does fate hand the speaker a lemon? How does she turn it into lemonade? Have you ever made lemonade out of a lemon? Explain.

Making Comparisons

Answer the questions about Dr. Bean, the doctor with Gaucher's disease, and Dr. Bradley, the osteopath you listened to in the previous two chapters. Then discuss their similarities and differences.

	Dr. Bean	Dr. Bradley
1. When did they decide to become doctors?		
2. Why did they become doctors?		
3. Who influenced their decisions?		
4. What other professions did they consider?		
5. What schools did they attend?		
6. Where were they originally from?		
7. What life-changing events did they experience?		

Further Study

Choose from the following.

1. Research Gaucher's disease or one of the following diseases that often afflicts a particular group. Write a one-page paper about the disease. You may also want to create a chart to show how the disease is genetically transmitted or who is likely to be afflicted.

    - breast cancer
    - diabetes
    - high-blood pressure (hypertension)
    - osteoporosis
    - sickle-cell anemia
    - Tay-Sachs disease

2. Research the Ronald McDonald House or a similar charity. Explain its purpose, whom it serves, where it is located, who funds the program, when it began, why it was started, and other important information. Write a short paper or make a presentation to the class.

 Web Activities

For additional activities related to this chapter, go to the *From College to Careers* website at **http://esl.college.hmco.com/students**.

CHAPTER 9
You Can Make a Difference

Heywood Sanders is the chairperson and a professor in the department of public administration at a large state university. As an urban affairs expert, Dr. Sanders' research on urban renewal and community development projects has been cited in professional literature, and he is frequently quoted by the news media.

Chapter Objectives

- Expressing goals and analyzing quotations
- Choosing the meaning
- Identifying definitions
- Listening for specific information
- Listening for irregular past tense
- Sharing ideas
- Building consensus
- Conducting research for a paper/presentation
- Making a presentation
- Writing a paper

Prelistening

Expressing Goals and Analyzing Quotations

Discuss the following questions.

1. What would you like to accomplish in your lifetime? What would you like to be remembered for? Why? How do you think you can make a difference in other people's lives? Explain.

2. What do you think the following two quotations mean? Do you agree with them? Why or why not?

   A winner never quits, and a quitter never wins.
   You can talk the talk, but can you walk the walk?

Vocabulary

Choosing the Meaning

Choose the most appropriate answer(s). More than one answer may be correct.

1. If you are taking a course in *urban planning,* you are learning how to _____.
   a. design a city
   b. organize your life
   c. plan a wedding

2. If someone has had a *remarkable* life, she has _____.
   a. done few great things
   b. done many great things
   c. yet to do anything great

3. If an area of a city has largely been *abandoned,* what has happened?
   a. People have moved out.
   b. Businesses have deserted the area.
   c. Houses have been rebuilt.

4. Many *developers* build _____.
   a. homes
   b. sandcastles
   c. office complexes

5. An *undesirable* area of a city is likely to have _____.
   a. a high crime rate
   b. some homeless people
   c. fancy hotels

6. Someone who has *committed* himself to doing something is _____.
   a. reluctant
   b. determined
   c. tired

7. Someone who *succeeded in* a task _____.
   a. failed
   b. did well
   c. needs to do it again

8. A city that is *losing its population* has _____.
   a. fewer people than before
   b. more people than before
   c. people who can't find their way back

9. Some people seem to be a *beacon of hope* by _____.
   a. never giving up
   b. being pessimistic
   c. being optimistic

10. What are you most likely to find in an *urban environment*?
    a. cars
    b. tall buildings
    c. cows

11. A city that is considered a *model* for other cities is _____.
    a. attractive
    b. an example
    c. unattractive

12. *Public housing projects* are built for the _____.
    a. affluent
    b. middle class
    c. poor

13. To build a *coalition*, it is important to be _____.
    a. indecisive
    b. cooperative
    c. confused

14. Which is the best example of *making a difference* in people's lives?
    a. receiving a pay increase
    b. being promoted
    c. finding a cure for cancer

Matching

Match the terms on the left with their definitions on the right.

_____ 1. associated with   a. regardless of
_____ 2. despite   b. uprisings
_____ 3. entire   c. linked to
_____ 4. obliged   d. compelled
_____ 5. riots   e. disagreeable
_____ 6. unpleasant   f. whole

Listening Comprehension Check

Listening for Specific Information

Listen to the recording. Then change the following statements to make them true.

1. The teacher's former student graduated from the University of Illinois, where she took courses in home economics.

   _____
   _____
   _____

2. Her first job after graduating was in Cleveland, where part of the city's historic Asian-American neighborhood had largely been abandoned in the late 1960s and early 1970s after a series of riots.

   _____
   _____
   _____

3. She worked on building a whole new office complex in a neighborhood in Cleveland.

4. She was unsuccessful in attracting people back to a city that a great many had given up on.

5. Cleveland and other older American cities were gaining population because people were searching for something newer and better and perhaps safer and more comfortable.

6. She later worked for the Department of the Interior in Washington, rebuilding federal public housing.

7. She is now in Denver creating a more pleasant urban environment and changing people's expectations by rebuilding some old federal public housing projects.

8. The professor is worried about his former student because she took the lessons of the classroom and the university and said that she was going to invest her life in making a real difference in people's lives.

Listening for Irregular Past Tense

The speaker uses past tense verbs to highlight the remarkable achievements of his former student. Listen again and write down as many past tense verbs as you can. Then circle the irregular verbs.

_____   _____   _____
_____   _____   _____
_____   _____   _____
_____   _____   _____
_____   _____   _____
_____   _____   _____

Discussion

Sharing Ideas

Discuss the following.

1. The speaker mentioned that his former student "took the lessons of the classroom and the university and said she was going to go invest her life in making a real difference in people's lives, and she has." Give examples of how you think she accomplished this goal. Talk about someone you know who has made a difference in the local community. How was this person able to make a difference?

2. Assisted by a developer, the woman "committed [herself] to building a whole new community" and succeeded in doing so. What are the major accomplishments in your life? Is there something important that you plan to commit yourself to? Explain.

3. *A winner never quits, and a quitter never wins.*
   You can talk the talk, but can you walk the walk?

   You read these expressions in the prelistening exercise. How does each apply to the woman?

Building Consensus

Look at the following list of famous people. Working in groups, choose the five who have had the greatest impact on the world. You must reach a consensus. Then explain your choices to the class. You may wish to add a name that is not on the list.

Aung San Suu Kyi	Sigmund Freud	Mother Teresa
Alexander Graham Bell	Galileo Galilei	Alfred Nobel
Simón Bolívar	Mahatma Gandhi	Louis Pasteur
César Chávez	Bill Gates	Pablo Picasso
Winston Churchill	Mikhail Gorbachev	Anwar el-Sadat
Confucius	Michael Jordan	Jonas Salk
Marie Curie	Martin Luther King Jr.	William Shakespeare
Charles Darwin	Leonardo da Vinci	Socrates
the Dalai Lama	Nelson Mandela	Stephen Spielberg
Amelia Earhart	Karl Marx	Harry Truman
Thomas Edison	Margaret Mead	Tzu Hsi
Albert Einstein	Golda Meir	Wilbur and Orville Wright
Henry Ford		

Further Study

Choose from the following.

1. From your group's list of the five most influential people, choose one person that you would like to learn more about. Research that person's life and write about the person's impact on the lives of others and the qualities that enabled this person to achieve success.

2. Research a specific riot and its impact on the surrounding neighborhood and on society in general. Here are some examples: Watts, 1965; French students, 1968; Kent State, 1970; LA (Los Angeles), 1991; World Trade Organization (WTO) in Seattle, 1999; and Iranian students, 2003. Be sure to find out what caused the riot and who was involved. Present your findings to the class.

Web Activities

For additional activities related to this chapter, go to the *From College to Careers* website at **http://esl.college.hmco.com/students**.

CHAPTER 10
I Fell in Love with the Natural Beauty

After working in the corporate world for several years in the United States and living in Latin America, Shannon Skaggs enrolled in a prestigious international graduate program and is pursuing a degree in business administration.

Chapter Objectives

- Sharing ideas
- Interviewing
- Identifying definitions
- Listening for information
- Listening for missing words
- Making inferences
- Expressing opinions
- Discussing advantages and disadvantages
- Conducting research for a presentation
- Interviewing
- Making a presentation

Prelistening

Sharing Ideas

Discuss the following with a partner.

1. What do these concepts mean to you? Define them in your own words.
   - a successful career
   - an ideal home and family

2. List the top five places in the world you dream of visiting some day. Explain to your partner why you'd like to visit these places.

Vocabulary

Interviewing

Fill in the chart by interviewing your classmates. Ask follow-up questions such as *What happened?*, *What kind?*, *When?*, and *Why?* The boldface words are used by the speaker.

Find someone who has . . .	Name
been **burnt out** from studying.	
had an **incredible** experience.	
participated in an unusual event.	
decided to study a third language.	
ridden in a **convertible**.	
volunteered to help with a good cause.	
experienced a **life-changing event**.	

Matching

Match the terms on the left with their definitions on the right.

_____ 1. befriended   a. a person who shows visitors around
_____ 2. furniture   b. became buddies with
_____ 3. guide (noun)   c. sofa, chair, bed
_____ 4. natural beauty   d. chance
_____ 5. opportunity   e. topography
_____ 6. originally   f. gifted, capable
_____ 7. outdoor lifestyle g. at first
_____ 8. talented   h. gorgeous scenery
_____ 9. terrain   i. hiking, camping, biking

Listening Comprehension Check

🎧 *Listening for Information*

Listen for and write information about the speaker's experiences in Chile. Then listen again and write details about her life in the United States.

Chile

Why she went: _____
_____
_____

What she liked: _____
_____
_____

Her first job: _____
_____
_____

Business opportunity: _____
_____
_____

United States

Job description: _____
_____
_____

City she lived in: _____
_____
_____

How old she was: _____
_____
_____

Things she sold: _____
_____
_____

Person she left: _____
_____
_____

Listening for Missing Words

Listen again and fill in the blanks with the missing words.

1. I just fell in love with the _____.

2. I decided to go back to Chile as a complete _____.

3. I was actually working in _____ management, which is like 401(k) plans and pension plans, and doing budgeting, forecasting, strategic planning for them and also managing their database.

4. It was a pretty heavy job, very _____.

5. I really did get _____.

6. I originally found a _____ position down there for an outdoor leadership school called NOLS, based in the U.S., but they have a _____ down there.

7. I just saw a great _____ to open the market for the Patagonians that don't know how to market tourism, but they sit on this beautiful land and have _____ cultural activities that you can _____ in.

Discussion

Making Inferences

1. Many Americans would admire the speaker's choice to quit her job and move to another country. Do you find this life change admirable? Why or why not? What do you think of a person who leaves everything behind to start anew? What can you infer about the speaker's personality?

2. Now discuss the speaker's personality in greater detail. Fill in the chart by placing a check mark in the **Yes** column if you think Shannon Skaggs possesses that particular trait; check **No** if you don't think she has that trait; check **Don't Know** if you can't tell. Then discuss your answers in a small group.

	Yes	No	Don't Know
adventurous			
ambitious			
bright			
cautious			
confident			
conservative			
fearless			
funny			
hesitant			
lackadaisical			
laid-back			
outgoing			
reserved			
restless			
shy			
wishy-washy			

3. Long work hours and too much stress can lead to job burnout. People who burn out may take some time off or change jobs or careers. Working with a partner, choose the three professionals from the following list who are most likely to burn out and the three who are least likely to burn out. Then discuss your reasons with another group.

accountant	firefighter	salesperson
computer scientist	lawyer	stockbroker
doctor	police officer	teacher
engineer	restaurant owner	writer
executive		

4. The speaker talks about her interest in helping to develop Patagonia's natural beauty for tourists. What are the advantages and disadvantages of this kind of tourism, known as ecotourism? Consider possible long-term effects—both positive and negative. Discuss the impact on the economy and the environment.

5. In the United States, the concept of surviving in the wilderness and testing oneself against nature is part of our cultural heritage. For this reason, many Americans pursue outdoor activities (e.g., hiking, camping, canoeing). What does this reveal about American culture? Do you have similar desires to explore the wild? Explain.

Further Study

Choose from the following.

1. Research NOLS (National Outdoor Leadership School) or another outdoor leadership school. Find out about the goals, purpose, cost, and other information you think is important. Report your findings to the class.

2. The speaker marveled at the beauty of Patagonia. Research Patagonia or another place known for its natural beauty. Then design a travel brochure promoting the tourist attractions. Share your brochure with the class.

3. Ask three people to discuss their ideas of the following:
   - a successful career
   - an ideal home and family

   Summarize your interviews for the class.

Web Activities

For additional activities related to this chapter, go to the *From College to Careers* website at http://esl.college.hmco.com/students.

CHAPTER 11
They Pay Me for This

The final speaker in this unit, Mark Schiff, talks about his unusual occupation. It will be up to you to guess what he does for a living.

Chapter Objectives

- Sharing opinions
- Creating a concept map
- Making deductions
- Listening for details
- Supporting opinions
- Interpreting quotations
- Expressing preferences
- Using *do* and *make*
- Researching and presenting a biographical sketch
- Reporting on or critiquing a movie, television show, and so on
- Telling a joke

Prelistening

Sharing Opinions

Discuss the following questions.

1. With a partner, list three occupations that you consider unusual. Create a class master list of all the occupational choices. Do you consider all these professions unusual? Why or why not?

2. Do you think your personality or culture affects what you find funny? Explain. What other factors influence what someone thinks is funny?

Creating a Concept Map

Concept maps help you visually organize your thoughts or questions by connecting ideas with lines or symbols to show their relationship to each other. They are commonly used as a brainstorming tool for giving speeches or writing papers.

Design a concept map about humor. Your map can be as simple or as elaborate as you choose. Then share this graphic organizer with a classmate.

To help you get started, here is a simple example of a concept map on a different topic.

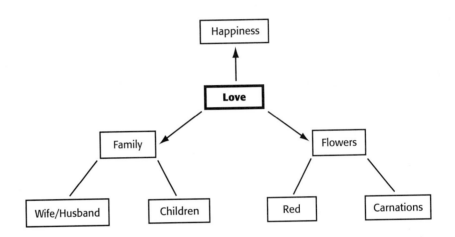

Compare your concept maps with a partner. How are your ideas different? How are they the same?

Listening Comprehension Check

Making Deductions

Designate a timekeeper who will record five-second increments on the board. As you listen to this recording, the speaker reveals information that gives you clues to his occupation. As soon as you think you know his occupation, write it down on the line labeled *1st guess* and record the time. Continue listening. If at any point you change your mind, record your new idea on the line marked *2nd guess*. Again, note the time.

1st guess _____ time _____

2nd guess _____ time _____

When you've finished listening, discuss the following questions with a partner.

1. At what point in the recording did you guess the speaker's correct occupation? If you changed your mind, at what point did you do so? Why?
2. What were the key words or other clues that helped you guess?
3. The speaker's occupation is a(n) _____.

Listening for Details

Listen again and answer the questions.

1. Mark Schiff emphasizes that he has never been late to a show even when he has had to travel great distances. He uses hours to indicate long-distance travel. What is the farthest that he has traveled to perform?

   _____
   _____
   _____

2. What two places did he get invited to perform for 15 minutes?

   _____
   _____
   _____

Discussion

Supporting Opinions

Discuss the following.

1. What do you think the speaker means by "the power of the joke, of laughter"?
2. What kind of prestige or cultural status does this occupation have? Would your family approve if you told them that you wanted to do the same thing? Why or why not?
3. Can jokes be universal or are they dependent on cultural context and language? Explain.
4. When do jokes cease to be funny and become stereotypes or prejudiced remarks? Has your own cultural/ethnic group been the brunt of a joke? How did you feel about it?

Interpreting Quotations

With a partner, discuss the following quotes. What do you think they mean? Give examples if possible.

> Humor is just another defense against the universe.—Mel Brooks
> Humor is a rubber sword; it allows you to make a point without drawing blood.—Mary Hirsch
> The human race has one really effective weapon, and that is laughter.
> —Mark Twain

The World's Funniest Joke

Do you know what the world's funniest joke is? The British Association for the Advancement of Science conducted a research project to find out. The Association received 40,000 jokes submitted over the Internet from seventy countries. In small groups, discuss six of the winning jokes and rank them in order from funniest to least funny. (The funniest should be ranked 1.) Then explain the reasons for your choices to the class.

_____ **A.** Two hunters are out in the woods when one of them collapses. He doesn't seem to be breathing, and his eyes are glazed. The other man pulls out his cell phone and calls emergency services. He gasps to the operator, "My friend is dead! What can I do?"

The operator, in a calm, soothing voice replies, "Take it easy. I can help. First, let's make sure he's dead."

There is a silence, then a shot is heard. Back on the phone, the guy says, "Ok, now what?"

_____ **B.** A man and a friend are playing golf one day at their local golf course. One of the guys is about to chip onto the green when he sees a long funeral procession on the road next to the course. He stops in mid-swing, takes off his golf cap, closes his eyes, and bows down in prayer.

His friend says, "Wow, that is the most thoughtful and touching thing I have ever seen. You truly are a kind man."

The man then replies, "Yeah, we were married 35 years."

_____ **C.** A woman gets on a bus with her baby. The bus driver says, "That's the ugliest baby that I've ever seen. Ugh!"

The woman goes to the rear of the bus and sits down, fuming. She says to a man next to her, "The driver just insulted me!"

The man says, "You go right up there and tell him off; go ahead, I'll hold your monkey for you."

_____ **D.** A doctor says to his patient, "I have bad news and worse news." "Oh dear, what's the bad news?" asks the patient.

The doctor replies, "You only have twenty-four hours to live."

That's terrible," said the patient. "How can the news possibly be worse?"

The doctor replies, "I've been trying to contact you since yesterday."

_____ **E.** Two guys are sitting on barstools. One starts to insult the other one. He screams, "I slept with your mother."

The bar gets quiet as everyone listens to see what the other weasel will do.

The first again yells, "I SLEPT WITH YOUR MOTHER!"

The other says, "Go home, Dad. You're drunk."

_____ **F.** "You're a high-priced lawyer. If I give you $500, will you answer two questions for me?"

"Absolutely! What's the second question?"

Do and Make

The speaker uses the phrases *do a show* and *do 15 minutes*. The use of *do* in English is often troublesome for nonnative speakers, as is differentiating between *do* and *make*. Read the examples of common ways that we use *do* and *make*.

*Do

To perform something (e.g., work, task, household chore)

- Do your homework.
- He can do twenty-five push-ups in thirty seconds.
- Always do your best.
- Can you do me a favor?
- I'm doing two shows tonight.
- After doing the dishes, you need to do the ironing.

Do lunch is a fairly recent expression in English, which means to have or to eat lunch with somebody.

Make

Create something or cause something to happen

- Hurry up! Make a decision.
- My friend wants to make a lot of money.
- I'm going to make a sandwich.

To force or to cause

- I can't make you work hard, but you should.
- Seeing my grandchildren this morning made my day.
- Practice makes perfect.

To reach

- She made her high school basketball team.
- I don't think that I can make it in time.
- We made it to the concert last night.

To gain or put forward

- He'll make a nice profit when he sells his house.
- Mr. Smith would like to make an offer.
- She will make two recommendations at the meeting.

LANGUAGE NOTE:

Noncount nouns do not have an indefinite article (*a* or *an*) preceding them (e.g., do homework, make money), but count nouns do have an indefinite article preceding them (e.g., do a favor, make a decision).

Fill in the blanks with the appropriate form of either *do* or *make*.

1. I have to _____ the laundry today.
2. The baby really _____ a mess.
3. Can I _____ a suggestion?
4. He must _____ ten years in prison for robbing the bank.
5. Let's _____ lunch sometime. I know of a great restaurant around the corner.
6. My husband's a great cook. He can _____ lunch for us.
7. The teacher _____ her tired students stand up and stretch.
8. I'm sure that your son will _____ a great lawyer.
9. Are you going to _____ another show? Your performances always _____ me laugh.

Further Study

Choose from the following.

1. Research the life of one of the following famous American comedians. Then give a brief biographical sketch to the class.

    Lenny Bruce   Phyllis Diller
    George Burns   Whoopi Goldberg
    George Carlin   Bob Hope
    Bill Cosby   Groucho Marx
    Sid Caesar   Eddie Murphy
    Billy Crystal   Paul Rodriguez
    Ellen DeGeneres   Jerry Seinfeld

2. Research the life of a comedian from a country other than the United States. Give a brief biographical sketch and an example of one of the comedian's famous lines or jokes.

3. Various types of entertainment can make you laugh. Pick one of the following to watch:
    - Comedy club performance
    - Movie—comedy
    - Theater production—comedy
    - TV show—sitcom

    Then choose *a* or *b*.

    a. Report to the class on the entertainment you watched. What was it about? How much did you understand? What, if anything, "tickled your funny bone" (made you laugh)?

    b. Imagine that you are a local entertainment critic. Write a review or critique. Scan the local newspaper for examples.

4. Tell a joke to the class that you think transcends culture. Why do you expect this joke to have universal appeal?

Web Activities

For additional activities related to this chapter, go to the *From College to Careers* website at **http://esl.college.hmco.com/students**.

UNIT 3

DON'T JUDGE A BOOK BY ITS COVER

Skills Chart

Listening	Speaking	Vocabulary	Integrated Skills
■ Listening for • information • ideas • the main idea • minimal encouragers • missing words • phrases • pronoun referents • details	■ Interviewing ■ Expressing opinions and preferences ■ Discussing quotations ■ Defending one side of an issue ■ Giving descriptions ■ Sharing ideas	■ Guessing meaning from context ■ Categorizing ■ Identifying definitions ■ Filling in the missing words ■ Guessing words	■ Building consensus ■ Analyzing stereotypes ■ Making inferences and comparisons ■ Synthesizing information ■ Sharing or writing a recipe ■ Creating an advertisement ■ Making a presentation ■ Writing about personal experiences

CHAPTER 12

Beauty Is in the Eye of the Beholder

David Marne is the owner of a real estate agency in a large city. He recalls his first day on the job.

> **Chapter Objectives**
>
> - Building consensus
> - Interviewing
> - Identifying definitions
> - Listening for information
> - Expressing ideas and preferences
> - Synthesizing information
> - Giving descriptions
> - Conducting research for a presentation
> - Compiling data
> - Making a presentation
> - Writing a report

Prelistening

Think / Pair / Share

Examine the list of features that people look for when shopping for a house and rank the top five to seven features according to your preferences. Then discuss your preferences with a partner. Create a new list of the top five to seven choices by reaching a consensus with your partner. Then share this list with another pair of students in your class.

_____	age of home	_____	potential resale value
_____	basement	_____	proximity to family members
_____	bedroom for each child	_____	room layout
_____	custom made	_____	safe neighborhood
_____	fenced yard	_____	two bathrooms
_____	gated community	_____	two stories
_____	large lot	_____	whatever spouse wants
_____	plenty of storage		

Vocabulary

Interviewing

Fill in the chart by interviewing your classmates. Ask the question, *Have you ever . . .* , following up with questions such as *When?* and *Why?* The boldface words are used by the speaker.

Have you ever . . .	Name
purchased something you couldn't afford?	
lived in a house with a **front porch**?	
given money to an **indigent** person?	
used too many minutes on your **cell phone**?	
thought you were **going to make it just on time** but then got **stuck** in traffic?	
told someone that you'd **be there in a second** when you didn't really mean it?	
looked up something on the Internet?	
lived **just around the corner** from a grocery store?	
worked for a large **firm**?	

Matching

Match the words and expressions on the left with their definitions on the right.

_____ 1. cracked in two   a. right in back of
_____ 2. directly behind   b. I didn't know
_____ 3. foundation   c. appearing lifeless
_____ 4. frequency   d. entered into the database
_____ 5. listed   e. supporting structure
_____ 6. naked   f. regularity
_____ 7. truly   g. broken in a couple of pieces
_____ 8. unbeknownst to me   h. a bad area of town
_____ 9. unconscious   i. honestly
_____ 10. wrong side of the tracks   j. without clothes

Listening Comprehension Check

Listening for Information

Listen and answer the following.

1. Place a checkmark next to the most appropriate titles for the recording.

    _____ Never Assume Anything
    _____ Expect the Unexpected
    _____ Secrets to Buying a Home
    _____ Life Is Full of Surprises
    _____ Leaving the Wrong Side of the Tracks

2. List the reasons the speaker thought the house would not sell and the reasons the house did sell.

Reasons House Would Not Sell	Reasons House Sold

3. The speaker says the unconscious man on the porch next door has "many empty bottles laying around him." What does this imply about the man?

_____

_____

_____

Discussion

Expressing Ideas and Preferences

Discuss the following.

1. Would you buy a house like the one that the speaker describes? Why or why not?

2. *Location, location, location* is a popular motto in the real estate business. What do you think this means? How does this apply to the situation described in the recording?

3. *One man's treasure is another man's junk.* What do you think this saying means? How does this relate to the story you just heard?

4. Study the floor plans and features of the houses. Decide which one you like the best. Discuss your preference with a classmate.

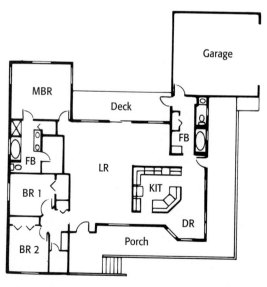

3 BR, 2 BA, LR, eat-in kitchen with new appl., sep. DR, large yard, nr. school

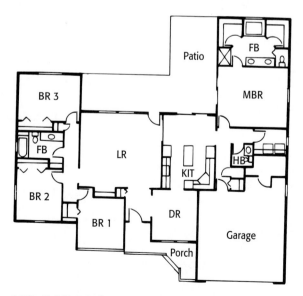

4 BR, 2 1/2 BA, lg. LR and DR, new elec., sec. system, patio, nr. shopping and walk to ocean

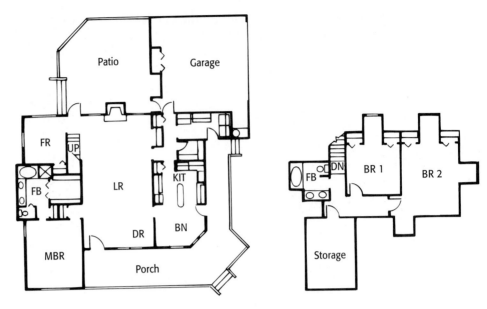

3 BR, 2 BA, LR, FR, lg. kitchen, 2 acs., lake view

Synthesizing Information

Discuss the following.

1. What kind of house would you expect for $40,000? What do you think is the average home price in the United States? In some cities, home prices are much higher than in others. What might contribute to this variation?

2. Look at the list of cities in different regions of the United States. Now match each city with what you think is the average home price in that city. Discuss the reasons for your selections.

_____ 1. Atlanta		a. $107,000
_____ 2. Chicago		b. $156,800
_____ 3. Honolulu		c. $263,300
_____ 4. New York		d. $392,200
_____ 5. Oklahoma City		e. $451,000
_____ 6. San Francisco		f. $647,300

Further Study

Choose from the following.

1. Ask two people to describe their neighborhood. Then ask them to talk about the features they like the most and the least. What would their ideal neighborhood be like? Write a brief report on your findings.

2. Using the list from the Prelistening activity, ask five people to rank their top five home features in order of importance. Which features were most popular? Least popular? Compile your data and report your findings to the class.

3. Refer to the list of cities in Synthesizing Information. Choose one of these cities or another large American city and research relocation information on the Internet. Prepare a report for the class on the cost of living and other factors to consider in deciding whether to move to that city.

4. Look for houses for sale in the newspaper and select one that is appealing to you. Describe the house to the class.

Web Activities

For additional activities related to this chapter, go to the *From College to Careers* website at **http://esl.college.hmco.com/students**.

CHAPTER 13

Never Assume Anything

You will now listen to two speakers, William King and Ruth Harwood, professors of business communication in a graduate program in international management. Both speakers specialize in crisis communication and conflict management.

Chapter Objectives

- Challenging your assumptions
- Categorizing
- Guessing meaning from context
- Filling in the missing words
- Listening for information and minimal encouragers
- Sharing ideas
- Building consensus
- Discussing quotations
- Writing about personal experiences
- Interviewing
- Conducting research for a presentation
- Making a presentation

Prelistening

Challenging Your Assumptions

Take the following quiz. Then compare your answers with that of a classmate. Next check your answers against those given in the appendix.

1. How long did the Hundred Years' War last?

_____

_____

2. Which country makes Panama hats?
   _____
   _____

3. From which animal do we get catgut?
   _____
   _____

4. What is a camel's hair brush made of?
   _____
   _____

5. What color is the male purple finch?
   _____
   _____

6. Where are Chinese gooseberries from?
   _____
   _____

7. What is the color of the black box in a commercial airplane?
   _____
   _____

8. What color is a U.S. green card (i.e., a resident alien card)?
   _____
   _____

9. Where are Jerusalem artichokes from?
   _____
   _____

10. The Canary Islands in the Atlantic Ocean are named after what animal?
    _____
    _____

How did you do? Did you think that the quiz was easy? Why or why not? Were you surprised at how well or how poorly you did? What assumptions did you make? Give examples.

Categorizing

Look at the following chart. Think about a classmate who is either a friend or someone you've talked to. Fill in the chart by making your best guesses about that person. Now interview that classmate and fill in the row marked "Actual Answer." Compare your guesses with the actual responses. What assumptions did you make? How accurate were your assumptions?

	Food Preferences	Study Habits	Hobbies	Dream Vacation	Main Things Looked for in a Hotel Room
Your Guess					
Actual Answer					

Vocabulary

Guessing Meaning from Context

Replace the underlined word(s) in each sentence with a word from the following list.

agenda critical satisfied
at stake parameters tendency
concern

1. The company's future is <u>in the balance</u>. If this deal falls through, we'll all lose our jobs.
2. It's <u>very important</u> that you do what the doctor tells you.
3. Even though he finished in second place, he was not <u>pleased</u> with the results.

4. Joe has a(n) <u>inclination</u> to speak before he thinks, which sometimes can be dangerous.
5. I can't let you do whatever you want; there will have to be certain <u>limits</u>.
6. I will not vote for him for president because I am concerned about his <u>program</u> for our country.
7. My son's poor grades are a real <u>worry</u> of mine.

Filling in the Missing Words

Fill in the blanks with the most appropriate words.

assume   crash in   perceptions
assumption   destination   perspective
cemented

1. Ever since my friend's son died, I have put my life in _____ and stopped being upset about minor things.
2. After working for twenty hours, I needed to find a bed to _____.
3. A scientist should avoid making a(n) _____ about the outcome of an experiment.
4. I know that your coworker said that she would complete the project by today, but you should never _____ anything.
5. People generally have negative _____ about him, but I never had any problems with him when I was his boss.
6. Los Angeles is my final _____.
7. After hours of negotiations, the diplomats finally _____ the deal.

Listening Comprehension Check

🎧 Listening for Information

Listen to the recording and answer the questions.

1. What do the students assume that the woman looks for in a hotel room?
   _____

2. What does the man think that she looks for?
   _____

3. What does the woman say that she actually looks for?
   _____

Listening for Minimal Encouragers

In addition to sounds such as *uh-huh* and *uhm*, the male speaker uses two of the following words to acknowledge that he understands and is listening to the female speaker. These words are called minimal encouragers. Listen again and circle the words that you hear.

go on	I see	okay
right	sure	really

Discussion

Sharing Ideas

Discuss the following.

1. What features do you look for in a hotel room? Why?
2. The main speaker says, "[We] have a tendency to look at it only from our own perspective." Do you agree? Why or why not?
3. What do you think the main speaker means by "cemented within your own parameters"?
4. Give an example of an instance in which an assumption you made was wrong. Be as specific as you can.
5. What assumptions do people make about you based on your appearance, ethnicity, or accent?

Think / Pair / Share

You have just won an all-expenses paid vacation to Hawaii. Here is a list of various features to consider in selecting your hotel room. Choose your top five preferences. Then share your list with a partner. Next combine your lists. You must reach a consensus. Finally, compare your new list with another pair of students in your class.

big bed	iron and ironing board
blow dryer	near ice machine
cable TV	newspaper delivered to the door
comfortable chair	nice view
elegant bathroom	no-smoking room
Internet hookup	room service

Discussing Quotations

These quotations are about misperceptions. Work with a partner to match the first part with the second part. Then choose one and discuss its meaning.

_____ 1. To spell out the obvious

_____ 2. Your understandings

_____ 3. What the caterpillar calls the end,

_____ 4. Worshipping the teapot

_____ 5. Assumptions allow the best in life

a. are of misunderstandings. —*St. Francis*

b. the rest of the world calls a butterfly.—*Lao Tzu*

c. is often to call it in(to) question.—*Eric Hoffer*

d. to pass you by.—*John Sayles*

e. instead of drinking the tea.—*Wei Wu Wei*

Completing Quotations

Finish the following quotations in your own words. Then compare your responses with the original quotations in the appendix.

1. We are entitled to make almost any reasonable assumption
   _____
   _____

2. Never assume,
   _____
   _____

3. Most of our assumptions
   _____
   _____

4. If we all worked on the assumption that what is accepted as true is really true,
   _____
   _____

Further Study

Choose from the following.

1. Write about your experiences living or traveling in another country. How did these experiences challenge your assumptions about that country and its people?

2. Ask someone to talk about what assumptions people make about them based on one or more of the following: culture, background, appearance, and accent. Report your findings to the class.

3. Research a scientific or historical assumption that has since been proven inaccurate (e.g., the earth is flat, the sun is at the center of the solar system, Manifest Destiny). How did people's knowledge, culture, and religion influence their thinking at the time? Report your findings to the class.

Web Activities

For additional activities related to this chapter, go to the *From College to Careers* website at **http://esl.college.hmco.com/students**.

CHAPTER 14 Computer Types

Pay close attention to Steven Dallenback, a computer scientist who works for a private research institute.

Chapter Objectives

- Analyzing stereotypes
- Completing a statement
- Identifying definitions
- Listening for missing words, phrases, and ideas
- Expressing opinions
- Conducting research for a presentation
- Interviewing
- Using a chart to make comparisons
- Making a presentation

Prelistening

Analyzing Stereotypes

Discuss the following.

People tend to generalize about the traits or characteristics of individuals in certain professions. For example, salespeople are often thought of as outgoing, aggressive, and unwilling to take no for an answer.

Write the stereotypes that you associate with each profession given in the chart. Then discuss how these stereotypes can be both positive and negative and how they can affect individuals in these professions. You may wish to discuss other professions not listed.

Profession	Stereotypes
accountant	
athlete	
computer scientist	
engineer	
flight attendant	
lawyer	
librarian	
nurse	
politician	
professor	

Completing a Statement

Refer to the stereotypes that you wrote about computer scientists in Analyzing Stereotypes. Then fill in the blanks in the following statements. Discuss your responses with a partner.

1. Computer scientists are typically _____.
2. They're not particularly _____.
3. Going to a party of computer scientists is _____.
4. They don't understand _____.

Vocabulary

Matching

Match the terms on the left with their definitions on the right.

_____	1. academic curricula	a.	communicating with
_____	2. bleak	b.	related professions
_____	3. goes back to	c.	forthcoming
_____	4. Hollywood	d.	movie industry
_____	5. interacting with	e.	sets of courses
_____	6. open	f.	normally
_____	7. parallel fields	g.	gloomy
_____	8. particularly	h.	represent
_____	9. portray	i.	especially
_____	10. typically	j.	experienced in a variety of activities
_____	11. well-rounded	k.	refers to

Listening Comprehension Check

CULTURAL NOTE:

Students who graduate from four-year colleges receive either a bachelor of arts (BA) degree or a bachelor of science (BS) degree. A BA tends to emphasize liberal arts courses (e.g., foreign languages, art, sociology, psychology, political science, and history), whereas a BS usually requires many science courses (e.g., biology, chemistry, engineering, computer science, and mathematics).

Listening for Missing Words

Listen to the recording and fill in the blanks with the missing words.
Note: The speaker's rate of speech is fast, so be prepared to listen to the recording several times.

1. Going to a party of computer scientists is pretty _____ sometimes.
2. They're not particularly _____.
3. They're typically _____.

Listening for Phrases

Listen again and complete the three phrases that include the word *social*. Then guess their meanings.

1. social _____

   Meaning: _____

2. social _____

   Meaning: _____

3. social _____

   Meaning: _____

Listening for Ideas

Listen again and circle the correct answer.

1. What is the speaker's point about Hollywood computer types?
   a. It is important to understand computers in the movie industry.
   b. Computer specialists are demanding more roles in movies.
   c. Don't ever give up dreaming of being a computer type in Hollywood.
   d. Computer scientists tend to be stereotyped in movies.

2. The speaker mentions that his wife _____.
   a. is also a computer nerd
   b. has given up on him ever becoming well rounded
   c. has a social sciences background
   d. loves him even though he's a computer scientist

3. One of the best things that ever happened to the speaker was _____.
   a. getting married
   b. becoming a computer scientist
   c. having to take liberal arts courses
   d. having to take computer courses

Discussion

Expressing Opinions

Discuss the following.

1. What do you think the speaker means when he says computer people are not particularly well rounded?

2. Do you agree with the speaker that attending a party with other computer scientists is bleak? Why or why not? What other professions are viewed in a similar way? Explain.

3. Think of a character in a television show or movie who is a computer nerd. Describe how the character is portrayed and discuss how the person fits or doesn't fit the stereotype.

4. What generalizations do people have of students in specific majors? (For example, medical students might be thought of as status conscious or interested in helping others.) You may want to refer to your notes from the prelistening activity. Do these stereotypes usually reflect people's views of professionals in those fields? Explain.

Further Study

Choose from the following.

1. Research a job that requires a computer science degree. Report on this job to the class. Include the following details in your report:
   - Responsibilities
   - Starting salary
   - Type of company that employs these professionals
   - Education requirements
   - Necessary experience
   - Location

2. Research two university catalogs to find out what courses are required for a BS in computer science. Compare the required courses in a chart. Report your findings to the class.

3. Talk to two people and ask them how their profession or major is stereotyped. Ask them to talk about how these stereotypes have impacted them. Report your findings to the class.

4. The speaker mentions that computer scientists are often stereotyped in movies. Watch a movie and report to the class on the portrayal of the main character's profession. Discuss whether this portrayal is realistic or stereotyped.

 ## Web Activities

For additional activities related to this chapter, go to the *From College to Careers* website at **http://esl.college.hmco.com/students**.

CHAPTER 15
Why Cake and the Japanese Market Don't Mix

Professor Lauranne Buchanan specializes in cross-cultural and marketing management, and she is on the editorial board of the *Journal of Marketing Research*.

Chapter Objectives

- Sharing ideas
- Answering questions
- Identifying definitions
- Guessing words
- Listening for the main idea and information
- Expressing opinions and making inferences
- Making comparisons
- Interviewing
- Compiling information
- Writing or sharing a recipe
- Gathering data
- Creating an advertisement
- Making a presentation

Prelistening

Sharing Ideas

Answer the following.

1. What foods do you typically associate with American culture? With other cultures?

   _____

   _____

   _____

2. What food was typically served in your household during your childhood? How often did you eat it? Who prepared it? What did you like or dislike about it?

_____

_____

_____

3. What's the most unusual food that you've ever eaten? Would you eat it again or do you still eat it? Why or why not?

_____

_____

_____

4. What are some popular desserts in the United States? Do you like these desserts? Would they be marketable in other countries? Why or why not?

_____

_____

_____

Answering Questions

Many foods that are popular in the United States came from other countries. Some of these foods are listed in the following chart. Answer the questions about each food. If you are unfamiliar with something, guess what you think it is (a main course, dessert, soup, fruit, grain, etc.) or ask a classmate for help. If you are not sure about where the food is from, refer to the list that follows the chart. Then compare your chart with someone else in your class.

Food	What Type of Food Is It?	Where Is It From?	Have You Tried It? (Yes/No)	Did You Like It? (Yes/No)
baklava				
borscht				
couscous				
curry				
enchilada				
kimchi				
kiwi				
lasagna				
sauerkraut				
soufflé				
sushi				

France
Germany
Greece
India
Italy
Japan
Korea
Mexico
New Zealand
North Africa
Russia

Vocabulary

Matching

Match the terms on the left with their definitions on the right.

_____ 1. did homework   a. concerns
_____ 2. oven   b. unsuccessful
_____ 3. product   c. satisfactory
_____ 4. failed   d. stove
_____ 5. issues   e. completed assignment
_____ 6. acceptable   f. primarily
_____ 7. mainly   g. merchandise

Guessing Words

Listen to the recording and fill in the chart.

Definition	Term Used in Recording
positive responses	
buyers	
first reaction	
housewives/househusbands	
the taste a particular food leaves in your mouth after swallowing it	

Listening Comprehension Check

Listening for the Main Idea

Choose the main idea of the recording.

a. Japanese companies face a variety of cultural issues when marketing a product in other parts of the world.
b. Persistence and research result in successful marketing in Japan.
c. Marketing a product in Japan can be thwarted by cultural barriers.
d. Rice is popular in Japan and so is cake, but rice cake is not.

Listening for Information

List the three problems that the speaker mentioned. The first one has been done for you.

Problem #1: No oven

Problem #2: _____

Problem #3: _____

What was the solution for the first problem?

_____

_____

_____

Discussion

Expressing Opinions and Making Inferences

Discuss the following.

1. Which country do you think the cake mix was from? What makes you think that it's from that country?

2. Why do you think that homemakers did not buy a second rice cooker solely for cakes?

3. Some foods are readily adopted into new cultures. For example, pizza originated in Italy but has become very American. Are there other foods that you think would be easily adopted in the United States? Can you think of any foods that would not be received well in the United States? In other countries? What cultural issues might make the difference between a food being a hit or a bust?

4. Convenience food such as frozen dinners, premade cookies, and cake mixes are common in the United States. What does this indicate about Americans' lifestyle and eating habits?

5. In the United States, fast food is popular because convenience and saving time often outweigh social or nutritional considerations. However, in some cultures, eating is considered an important social event. Which do you prefer? Why?

6. How do desserts in the United States compare to desserts in other countries? How does breakfast in the United States compare to breakfast in other countries?

Further Study

Choose from the following.

1. Ask five people what their favorite food is. Then compile the information as a class. What did your survey indicate was the most popular food?

2. Find or write a recipe for an interesting or unusual food. If possible, cook the food and share it with the class. Bring copies of the recipe for your classmates.

3. Go to a supermarket and list the types of cake mixes available. Include information such as flavors, ease of preparation, prices, and so on. Jot down anything surprising or unusual. Report your findings to the class.

4. Create an advertisement for an unusual food. Think about your target audience or market. Present it to the class. Then have your classmates critique the commercial.

 ## Web Activities

For additional activities related to this chapter, go to the *From College to Careers* website at **http://esl.college.hmco.com/students**.

CHAPTER 16: The Emerging Hispanic Market

Humberto Valencia is a professor of marketing. Dr. Valencia's areas of expertise include marketing to Hispanics in the United States, cross-cultural consumer behavior research, and advertising in Latin America. Dr. Valencia came to the United States from Peru.

Chapter Objectives

- Expressing opinions
- Listening for missing words
- Listening for details
- Analyzing ideas and expressing opinions
- Describing a commercial
- Conducting research for a presentation
- Creating a graph
- Making a presentation
- Defending one side of an issue

Prelistening

Expressing Opinions

Answer the following.

1. What do you think it means to be bilingual-bicultural?

    _____
    _____
    _____

2. What does the term *Hispanic* mean? How have you heard it used?

   _____
   _____
   _____

3. Why do you think the Hispanic market is becoming more and more important to advertisers in the United States?

   _____
   _____
   _____

4. Describe your favorite television commercial. What product or service does it sell? What market does it target?

   _____
   _____
   _____

5. What do you think are some key markets that advertisers target? What types of products or services are marketed to these groups (e.g., video games for teenagers)?

   _____
   _____
   _____

6. Why do you think it is so important for advertisers to extensively research a market? What are the possible consequences if they don't?

   _____
   _____
   _____

LANGUAGE NOTE:

The speaker uses the term *market* to refer to potential customers for a particular product or service. There are many different markets (e.g., male market, youth market, white-collar market). *Market* is also used as a verb to mean the business activities of promoting, selling, and distributing a product or service to potential customers in a way that makes people eager to buy that product or service. Here's an example: The company is marketing our new line of cosmetics to women of color.

Listening Comprehension Check

Listening for Missing Words

Listen to the recording and fill in the missing words. Then guess their meanings.

. . . if you really want to (1) _____ to these Hispanics, you have to speak to them in their own language, in Spanish, because you have a (2) _____ of the market that is Spanish-language (3) _____.
In other words, they speak very little English or no English—maybe because they're fresh (4) _____, maybe because. . .
And then you got the bilingual-bicultural like myself who are (5) _____ in both languages.

Listening for Details

Read the following questions. Then listen to the recording and circle the correct answer. More than one answer may be correct.

1. What are some of the reasons given why Hispanics belonging to the Spanish-language-dominant group do not speak English?
   a. They are fresh (new) immigrants.
   b. They don't care to learn English.
   c. They are unable to learn English.
   d. They don't need to learn English.

2. In which cities can Spanish speakers survive without speaking English?
   a. Miami
   b. Los Angeles
   c. Las Vegas
   d. San Antonio

3. Which of the following groups does the speaker mention?
   a. Spanish-language dominant
   b. bilingual–bicultural
   c. English-language dominant

4. Read the following excerpt from the recording. *It is argued that if you want to reach their heads, you can speak to them in English. If you want to reach their hearts, then you've got to speak to them in Spanish.* Who do the pronouns *you*, *their*, and *them* refer to?
   a. *You* refers to advertisers.
   b. *You* refers to teachers.
   c. *Their* and *them* refer to Hispanics and Hispanic Americans.
   d. *Their* and *them* refer to husbands and wives.

Discussion

Analyzing Ideas and Expressing Opinions

Discuss the following.

1. In the quotation from Listening for Details (no. 4), what do you think it means to appeal to someone's heart? To someone's head?

2. Do you have to immigrate to another country to consider yourself bicultural? How has your own cultural identity been influenced by learning another language or living in another culture? How has your understanding of English affected your understanding of the United States? Has your exposure to another language and culture affected how you view yourself in relation to your home culture? Explain.

3. In some urban centers in the United States (e.g., Chicago, New York, Houston, Los Angeles), some immigrants settle in neighborhoods where their home language and culture are easily maintained, making it unnecessary for the immigrants to learn English. What role, if any, do you feel these neighborhoods play in transitioning people from their home culture to their target culture? How do you think these neighborhoods have been important to immigrants? Why do some groups tend to assimilate more easily into American culture than other groups?

4. America has been referred to as both a melting pot and a salad bowl. How do you think these descriptions apply to the groups characterized by the speaker? Which do you think best describes immigrants to the United States? Why?

5. Which ethnic groups in the United States do you think are important targets for advertisers? Explain.

Further Study

Choose from the following.

1. Look at several different magazine ads. Bring in an ad that appeals to the heart and one that appeals to the head. Explain each ad's appeal.

2. Research the Hispanic population's growth in the last twenty years in the United States using either national, state, or local statistics. Create a graph that depicts the changes. If you prefer, you may choose a different ethnic group to research. Present your findings to the class.

3. Did you know that the United States does not have an official language? Research the arguments for and against making English the official language. Be prepared to defend one side.

4. In the United States, a census is conducted every ten years. The form used by the U.S. Census Bureau is printed in many languages to accommodate the diversity represented in this country. Find out which languages the census form is printed in. Then list all the home languages that are spoken by your classmates. Next use this information along with your research on the census to present a report to the class. Be sure to mention whether your classmates could get a copy of the census in their native languages.

5. Find information on election ballots printed for statewide elections in California or another state with a large and diverse immigrant population (e.g., New York, Florida, Illinois). Report on the following:

   - the number of languages the ballots are printed in
   - which languages the ballots are printed in
   - procedures for requesting a ballot in another language (e.g., requesting ballots ahead of time or at a polling place)
   - availability of an interpreter (If an interpreter is available, who absorbs the cost?)

Web Activities

For additional activities related to this chapter, go to the *From College to Careers* website at **http://esl.college.hmco.com/students**.

UNIT 4

CROSS-CULTURAL MISCOMMUNICATION

Skills Chart

Listening	Speaking	Vocabulary	Integrated Skills

■ Listening for
  • information
  • descriptions
  • examples
  • missing words
  • ideas
■ Listening globally
■ Choosing a summary
	■ Interviewing
	■ Expressing and soliciting opinions
	■ Sharing ideas, information, and cultural perspectives
	■ Discussing cultural faux pas, assumptions, gestures, cultural time concepts, and quotations
		■ Making word associations
		■ Filling in the missing words
		■ Using phrasal verbs
		■ Using expressions
		■ Identifying definitions
			■ Making comparisons and inferences
			■ Analyzing gestures, connotations, and situations
			■ Synthesizing information
			■ Role-playing
			■ Using a timeline to report information
			■ Hypothesizing
			■ Making a presentation
			■ Writing a cultural story

CHAPTER 17
Everything Is NOT Okay

Dr. Roy Nelson, a professor of international studies, is the first speaker in this unit to address cross-cultural miscommunication. Dr. Nelson has conducted market research for pharmaceutical companies in Brazil. He has also served as a consultant to the World Bank and has conducted research in Argentina, Venezuela, and other Latin American countries.

Chapter Objectives

- Analyzing gestures
- Filling in the missing words
- Listening for information and making inferences
- Choosing a summary
- Role-playing and discussing cultural faux pas
- Reading and writing a critique
- Role-playing miscommunication
- Interviewing

Prelistening

Discussing Gestures

Match the gesture on the left side of the chart with its U.S. meaning on the right side. Which of the gestures have you seen Americans use? In what situations were they used? Does the gesture have a different meaning in your culture? If so, what does it mean?

_____ 1. circle made with thumb and index finger

a. greeting between friends or people who meet for the first time

_____ 2. shaking hands

b. A-okay sign; Everything's good.

_____ 3. exchange of kisses on the cheek

c. carries no message

_____ 4. hitting the forehead with the palm of the hand

d. bad; I don't like it.

_____ 5. making a spinning motion with index finger next to your temple

e. Come here.

_____ 6. beckoning with the palm up

f. I forgot.

_____ 7. thumbs-down

g. crazy

_____ 8. exposing the sole of one's shoe

h. the way some family members greet each other

Vocabulary

Filling in the Missing Words

Fill in the blanks with the most appropriate words.

correct	just
fancy	sir
faux pas	snobbish
had no idea	stomped off
insulted/offended	terrible

1. He is so _____ that he does not talk to anyone who makes less money than he does.
2. I _____ that he was a VIP (very important person). If I had known, I would have treated him better.
3. I want to take my wife to a _____ restaurant for our twenty-fifth anniversary.
4. John was so angry with his boss that he refused to do any more work and _____.
5. You _____ missed him. He left a minute ago.
6. Fred did such a _____ job, I had to fire him.
7. Not taking off your shoes when entering a home is a _____ in Japan.
8. Paolo was _____ when someone criticized his mother.
9. Maria was the only student to get all the answers _____ on the exam.
10. _____ is a polite form of address.

Listening Comprehension Check

Listening for Information and Making Inferences

Listen to the recording and answer the questions.

1. What gesture did the speaker use that caused miscommunication?

2. How did the speaker describe the waiter?

3. Why was the waiter insulted?

4. What is the proper okay sign in Brazil?
   _____

5. How long do you think the speaker had been in Brazil when he offended the waiter? Why do you think so?
   _____

6. How good do you think the speaker's Portuguese was? Why?
   _____

7. Where is the speaker from? How do you know?
   _____

Choosing a Summary

Choose the best summary.

a. The speaker ate in a fancy restaurant and was insulted by a waiter who had used an offensive gesture.

b. The speaker was a waiter in Brazil and was offended by an American-style okay sign.

c. When the speaker was eating in a fancy restaurant, he offended a snobby waiter with a hand gesture.

d. A snobbish waiter in Brazil gave the speaker a thumbs-up sign and stomped off.

Discussion

Role-Playing and Discussing Cultural Faux Pas

Discuss the following.

1. Discuss the relationship and expected behavior of customers and waiters in a restaurant. How are these expectations different from country to country? How would *you* get a waiter's attention, and how would *you* indicate that you are enjoying your meal? With a partner, role-play a customer and a waiter. Demonstrate a polite exchange or a situation that might cause confusion or misunderstanding (include gestures if possible).

2. A cultural faux pas is sometimes unavoidable when visiting another country. Discuss a cultural faux pas you or someone you know committed in another country. What happened? Describe people's reactions.

Further Study

Choose from the following.

1. Thumbs-up and thumbs-down signs are sometimes used to express a critic's opinion of a movie, a concert, or a restaurant. With a partner, complete the following steps:
   - Go to a movie, concert, or restaurant.
   - Read some critiques from the newspaper.
   - Prepare a critique using a similar style.
   - Present your critique to the class.
   - Have your classmates guess whether you would give the movie, concert, or restaurant a thumbs-up or thumbs-down and why.

2. As Dr. Nelson suggests, when traveling in another country, people can find themselves in uncomfortable situations due to misinterpreting nonverbal communication. With your partner, role-play a situation in which misinterpreting a gesture or other form of nonverbal communication causes miscommunication.

3. Watch five or ten minutes of a television program with the sound turned off. Note the gestures and other forms of nonverbal communication. Guess what the story is about based on your observations of the body language and gestures of the characters. Now watch the rest of the show with the sound turned on. Was your guess about the storyline correct? Report your analysis to the class. Include the name and type of program.

4. Ask three people from different countries for the two most important things you need to know about their cultures in order to avoid a cultural faux pas. Report your findings to the class.

Web Activities

For additional activities related to this chapter, go to the *From College to Careers* website at **http://esl.college.hmco.com/students**.

CHAPTER 18
The Spirit of African Hospitality

Olufemi Babarinde discusses cross-cultural miscommunication on another continent. Professor Babarinde specializes in international political economy and development. His main areas of expertise include Europe and Sub-Saharan Africa. Dr. Babarinde emigrated from Nigeria.

Chapter Objectives

- Hypothesizing
- Answering questions
- Identifying definitions
- Making word associations
- Listening for information
- Choosing a summary
- Listening for missing words
- Expressing opinions
- Discussing advantages and disadvantages
- Writing a cultural story
- Interviewing
- Making a presentation

Prelistening

Hypothesizing

Imagine that you are an exchange student living abroad for a year, and your host family owns a house pet. With a partner, discuss which of these pets you would feel the most comfortable and least comfortable living with. Then share your opinions with the class.

cat	goat	rabbit	snake
dog	goldfish	rooster	turtle
ferret	hamster		

Africa Quiz

How much do you know about Africa? Test your knowledge by answering as many questions as you can. Then check your answers against those listed in the appendix.

1. What is the largest country in Africa?

2. What is the smallest country in Africa?

3. What is the most populous city?

4. What are the two major religions?

5. How many ethnic groups are there?

6. What is the most populous country?

7. What is the world's longest river?

8. What is the world's largest desert (with an area greater than the continental United States)?

9. Which country has the longest tradition of independent statehood?

10. How many languages are spoken?

Vocabulary

Matching

Match the terms on the left with their definitions on the right.

_____ 1. duration   a. crying
_____ 2. hosted   b. a person you share living quarters with
_____ 3. lexicon   c. offered hospitality
_____ 4. pet   d. length of time
_____ 5. roommate   e. the feeling characterizing something
_____ 6. sobbing   f. however
_____ 7. spirit of   g. an animal kept for companionship
_____ 8. whereas   h. vocabulary

Making Word Associations

In each row, cross out the term that does not relate to the boldface word.

1. **affection**	liking	wealth	fondness
2. **celebrating**	partying	studying	having fun
3. **classic**	atypical	standard	regular
4. **confused**	puzzled	bewildered	organized
5. **commonly**	frequently	stubbornly	normally
6. **concerned**	tired	worried	anxious
7. **distraught**	troubled	disoriented	distressed
8. **honorable**	pushy	respectable	proper
9. **hospitality**	kindness	sickness	generosity
10. **meal**	lunch	dinner	exercise
11. **rooster**	hen	dog	chicken
12. **unusually**	sincerely	strangely	abnormally

FROM COLLEGE TO CAREERS: The Spirit of African Hospitality

Listening Comprehension Check

Listening for Information

Listen to the recording and answer the questions.

1. Why is the young woman staying with the family in Africa?
   _____

2. According to the speaker, which of the following is an African perspective?
   a. Only blood relatives are truly like family.
   b. Anyone the age of their child is truly like family.
   c. Children should respect their aunts and uncles.

3. What did the family give the student to make her feel more at home?
   _____

4. What did the family serve at the student's farewell dinner?
   _____

5. How did the student react to the family's gesture? Explain.
   _____

6. Why was the family confused about the student's reaction?
   _____

CULTURAL NOTE:

The speaker began with the words *Once upon a time*. He uses this introduction to indicate that he is going to tell a story.

Choosing a Summary

Choose the best summary.

a. Once upon a time an American girl went to Africa and took her pet rooster with her. The two were inseparable. She and her pet were adopted by an African family. One day the rooster ran away, which upset the girl. To console her, the host family prepared a special meal.

b. Once upon a time an American girl and her pet rooster moved to Africa. They lived with a host family. One evening the girl brought her pet to dinner with her, which offended the family members because they didn't allow pets at the table.

c. Once upon a time an American girl went to Africa as an exchange student. She received a pet rooster from her host family. When she was ready to leave, her host family served her the pet for dinner. The girl was upset, and the family was confused.

d. Once upon a time an American girl hosted an African exchange student. The student was shocked that the American kept a chicken as a pet. One day the chicken crossed the road and was hit by a car. This saddened the girl, who then invited the exchange student to a dinner in honor of the departed chicken.

Listening for Missing Words

Listen again and fill in the missing words.

broached the subject
eve of her departure
in any case
it was a pity

took a liking to
to that end
you can only imagine

1. But _____, what happened was that they _____ to this lady.
2. And _____, they gave her a rooster.
3. On the _____, the family had a meal for her, a special meal, and so forth.
4. In the course of the dinner, she found out, she _____ of what would happen to her pet.
5. _____ she couldn't carry the pet with her back to the States.
6. So _____ how distraught she was.

Discussion

Expressing Opinions

Discuss the following.

1. The speaker explains how the exchange student's host family honored her with a special meal. How would you honor someone who's been a guest at your home?

2. How much do you think the exchange student understood about her host culture? Explain.

3. Imagine that you are going to be an exchange student in Africa. Where in Africa would you like to live? Why? What cultural differences might be challenging for you? Explain.

4. In the United States, *a dog is man's best friend* is a popular saying. What do you think this saying means? Why do you think pets are often treated like members of the family in the United States?

5. Talk about your own pet(s) and what the advantages and disadvantages are of owning a pet.

Further Study

Choose from the following.

1. Write a story that demonstrates a cultural point. Write it in the classic style—*Once upon a time* . . . . You may retell a traditional story or create your own story.

2. Ask three people who have pets the following questions:
   - How many pets do you have?
   - What kind of pets do you have?
   - What do you feed your pets?
   - Do you consider your pets part of the family? Why?
   - Do you take your pets with you when you go places?

   Report your findings to the class.

3. Research an African country of your choice and present information on this country to the class. Include information on the culture, ethnic groups, major religions, common languages, and food.

4. Research an international student exchange program. Find out about the countries involved, how long the program lasts, and what requirements students must meet to take part in the program. Summarize your research for the class and explain why it appeals to you.

Web Activities

For additional activities related to this chapter, go to the *From College to Careers* website at **http://esl.college.hmco.com/students**.

CHAPTER 19

It's Cool to Be Late

Dr. Humberto Valencia gives some examples of cross-cultural miscommunication that result from different interpretations of time.

Chapter Objectives

- Discussing cultural time concepts
- Making word associations
- Listening globally
- Listening for information
- Making comparisons
- Discussing assumptions
- Using phrasal verbs
- Interviewing
- Synthesizing information
- Using a timeline to report information
- Collecting data on television commercials
- Making a presentation

Prelistening

Discussing Cultural Time Concepts

Discuss the following.

1. Time is relative. Cultural expectations as well as the type of event dictate the arrival time individuals consider most appropriate. How do you think culture and personality affect people's perceptions of time?

2. Look at the following list of events. Consider the type of event and the scheduled time. Mark your ideal arrival time on each timeline. Then indicate the time that you would consider too early and too late to arrive at the event. Share your timelines with a partner and discuss any differences.

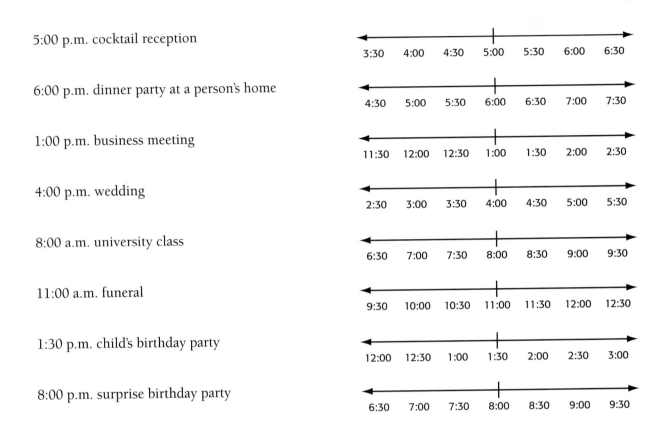

5:00 p.m. cocktail reception

6:00 p.m. dinner party at a person's home

1:00 p.m. business meeting

4:00 p.m. wedding

8:00 a.m. university class

11:00 a.m. funeral

1:30 p.m. child's birthday party

8:00 p.m. surprise birthday party

Vocabulary

Making Word Associations

In each row, cross out the term that does not relate to the boldface word.

1. **ceremony**	service	observance	formal procedure	informal procedure
2. **mandatory**	optional	required	obligatory	compulsory
3. **overtly**	obviously	openly	clearly	secretly
4. **yelling**	shouting	whispering	screaming	hollering

Listening Comprehension Check

> **LANGUAGE NOTE:**
>
> In this segment, the speaker describes a commercial targeted at a Hispanic, or Latino, audience. Note that the speaker uses the words *ad* (short for advertisement) and *commercial* interchangeably. He implies that the advertisement is on television by using the word *commercial* and through his description.

Listening Globally

Listen to the recording.

1. Circle the statement that best describes the first part of this recording.

    a. The speaker describes a commercial in which two cultural mistakes occur.

    b. The speaker recommends that wives not shout at their husbands.

    c. The speaker describes the emerging Hispanic market in the United States.

    d. According to the speaker, being late is not very cool.

2. Circle the statement that best describes the second part of this recording.

    a. The speaker describes the complications of planning a wedding.

    b. The speaker describes different cultural ideas of time.

    c. According to the speaker, cross-cultural marriages are challenging.

    d. The speaker believes that time is irrelevant.

Listening for Information

Listen again and answer the questions.

1. What were the two mistakes in the commercial? Why were they mistakes?

    _____
    _____
    _____

2. The speaker gave an example of a wedding ceremony between a Cuban American and a non-Cuban American in Miami scheduled for 6:00. Which group received invitations for 5:00 and which group got invitations for 6:00? Why?

    _____
    _____
    _____

Discussion

Making Comparisons

Discuss the following.

1. As mentioned by the speaker, the concept of time differs among cultures. Work with a partner from a culture other than your own. If you and your partner think an expression or statement is generally true about the United States, place a check mark under the heading *United States* in the chart. Then ask your partner which statements are generally true about his or her culture. If a statement is true, place a check mark under the heading *Partner's Culture*. Then complete the process for your own culture in the column labeled *My Culture*. Finally, compare your responses with another pair of students in your class.

	United States	Partner's Culture	My Culture
1. Time is money.			
2. Being late to a business meeting shows that you are not reliable.			
3. Time is a servant, not a master.			
4. It is impolite to show up on time for a dinner party.			
5. It's cool to be late.			
6. Don't put off until tomorrow what you can do today.			
7. The early bird gets the worm.			
8. Slow and steady wins the race.			

2. Share an anecdote about timeliness or being late.

3. What does the speaker mean by *it's cool to be late*? Do you agree? Why or why not? Give an example to support your view.

Discussing Assumptions

Discuss the following.

1. What does the speaker mean by a *male-dominated society*? As an example, the speaker mentions that a woman would not shout at her husband in a male-dominated society. Give another example of a type of behavior that you think would not be acceptable in a male-dominated culture.

2. Indicate which of the following statements are appropriate actions in your culture by writing *A* for acceptable and *U* for unacceptable. Then compare your answers with those of a classmate.

    _____ a. A husband quits his job to stay at home with the kids because his wife makes more money than he does.

    _____ b. A husband refuses to do the laundry because he claims that it is his wife's job.

    _____ c. A husband volunteers his wife to prepare dinner for his boss without consulting with her first.

    _____ d. A husband goes out to a bar with his boss after work without asking his wife.

    _____ e. A father refuses to allow his son to study ballet.

Phrasal Verbs

The speaker uses the phrasal verb *show up* several times. Phrasal verbs, also called two-word verbs, are frequently used in conversation. Complete each sentence using the most appropriate phrasal verb listed. Change the tense of the phrasal verb when necessary.

catch up   lighten up
freeze up   make up
freshen up   show up
get up   split up
keep up   throw up

1. Let's _____ into groups.

2. Don't be so stressed out about the class. You'll do fine. _____, would you?

3. The teacher talks so quickly in class, I can't _____.
4. I missed class yesterday, so I had to _____ my work.
5. I studied and practiced very hard for my presentation, but when I finally got in front of the class, I simply _____.
6. I have to _____ at 5:30 every morning so that I can be at work by 6:45.
7. Dinner was at 6:00, but he didn't _____ until 7:00.
8. He _____ after eating twelve hot dogs.
9. Carla was in second place until the last mile, when she finally _____ to the leader.
10. I was up all night studying. Before I meet my friends, I need to _____.

Further Study

Choose from the following.

1. Select a culture other than your own and investigate the time concepts common to that culture. Consider how the perception of time may differ depending on the situation (e.g., business meeting, social events). Refer to the prelistening activity at the beginning of this chapter for more ideas. Share your findings with the class.

2. Use a timeline similar to the one in the prelistening activity to gather data from three people outside your class. Combine your findings with another student and report them to the class.

3. Watch thirty minutes of television and record the types of advertisements you see. Be sure to note the station and program that you watched. (You may wish to record the program.) Use the data that you gathered and report on the commercials that you liked the most and the least. Explain your choices.

	Product or Service	**Market** (Target Audience)	**Your Opinion** (e.g., funny, culturally inappropriate, makes you want to buy this product)
Ad #1			
Ad #2			
Ad #3			
Ad #4			

Web Activities

For additional activities related to this chapter, go to the *From College to Careers* website at **http://esl.college.hmco.com/students**.

CHAPTER 20: What Part of NO Don't You Understand?

Dr. Roy Nelson provides an example of cross-cultural miscommunication in another part of the Americas.

Chapter Objectives

- Analyzing connotations
- Filling in the missing words
- Listening for descriptions and examples
- Listening for information
- Sharing ideas
- Gathering information
- Soliciting opinions

Prelistening

Analyzing Connotations

In the recording, the speaker says, "People don't want to necessarily say no." The following are various phrases that can mean no. Some are polite, others are impolite, and some could be either depending on the situation and the speaker's tone of voice. Write *P* if you think the answer is polite, *I* if you believe it is impolite, or *B* if both could apply. Then compare your answers with those of a classmate. (See the Language Note in Chapter 23 for more information on connotations.)

_____ 1. Maybe.
_____ 2. No, I'm not interested.
_____ 3. Let me think about it.
_____ 4. No way.
_____ 5. I'll get back with you on that.
_____ 6. Not at the moment.

_____ 7. Not in a million years.
_____ 8. I don't think so.
_____ 9. Absolutely not.
_____ 10. That's a possibility.
_____ 11. Some other time.
_____ 12. I'll take a rain check.

Vocabulary

Filling in the Missing Words

Fill in the blanks with the most appropriate words.

backed up	Jeep
clearly	mechanic
executive	necessarily
happiness	prepared
it turns out	throughout

1. Just because he said yes doesn't _____ mean he agrees with you.
2. It _____ wasn't your fault.
3. I hope that your new bride brings you many years of _____.
4. I've used the same _____ to repair my car for years. He always finds the problem with my vehicle.
5. I'm sorry I can't meet you for lunch, but I'm so _____ with work.
6. Everyone thought Mr. Morgan was honest, but _____ that he stole money from many people.
7. She is _____ to compete in the marathon.
8. She likes to drive her _____ in the summer.
9. A(n) _____ of a company must make many important decisions.
10. I will have to check up on my baby _____ the night.

> **LANGUAGE NOTE:**
>
> The word *necessarily* is used with a negative to soften the message. For example: *Money doesn't necessarily buy happiness. What he said is not necessarily correct.*

Listening Comprehension Check

Listening for Descriptions and Examples

Listen to the recording and answer the questions.

1. What's the speaker's first example of someone saying *yes* when he means *no*?
   _____
   _____

2. How does the speaker describe Latin American culture?
   _____
   _____

3. Circle the days that the mechanic says the customer will be happy.
   Monday   Tuesday   Wednesday   Thursday   Friday

Listening for Information

Listen and circle the correct answer.

1. When did the customer initially think the car would be ready?
   a. next week
   b. on Friday
   c. on Monday

2. Which of the following was the mechanic's response to the customer's first question?
   a. I'll have it ready as you requested.
   b. It won't be ready until Monday.
   c. Call me back and confirm the time.

3. Which of the following did the customer ask?
   a. Why did you tell me the car would be ready next week?
   b. Why did you tell me that it would be ready on Friday when clearly it wouldn't be?
   c. I am a good customer; why did you lie to me?

4. Why did the mechanic give an inaccurate time frame?
   a. He wanted the customer to be upset.
   b. He didn't care about the customer's schedule.
   c. He wanted the customer to be happy for as long as possible.

Discussion

Sharing Ideas

Discuss the following.

1. How would you have reacted to the mechanic's explanation if it had been your car that was delayed?
2. Why do you think the speaker says that the Latin American culture is nonconfrontational? What do you think it means to be nonconfrontational?
3. *Ignorance is bliss.* What do you think this expression means? How does it apply to the situation in the recording?

Further Study

Choose from the following.

1. Call a mechanic and provide the make, model, and year of your car (or a car you would like to drive). Then ask about the following:
   - The time required to do a specific type of repair (e.g., front-end alignment, tune-up, oil change, timing belt replacement)
   - Whether you need to schedule an appointment
   - Methods of payment accepted

   Report your findings to the class.

2. Complete one of the following tasks.
   a. Using the list of phrases from the prelistening activity, ask three native speakers which answers are polite and which are impolite. Also ask them to add other phrases. Report your findings to the class.
   b. Go to a place where people gather (e.g., cafeteria, information desk) and listen for different ways that people say yes or no. Report your findings to the class.

Web Activities

For additional activities related to this chapter, go to the *From College to Careers* website at **http://esl.college.hmco.com/students**.

CHAPTER 21
It's All about the Contract

Shannon Skaggs shares her first-hand experiences with cultural differences in business practices.

Chapter Objectives

- Sharing cultural perspectives
- Sharing personal information
- Identifying definitions
- Filling in the missing words
- Listening for information and ideas
- Analyzing situations and discussing quotations
- Using expressions
- Making comparisons
- Writing sentences using expressions
- Making a presentation

Prelistening

Sharing Cultural Perspectives

With a partner, discuss under what circumstances it is acceptable to ask the following questions. Consider who you're talking to and how well you know the person, and other factors. For example, in American culture it is acceptable for an adult to ask a child, "How old are you?" However, adults do not usually ask this of each other.

1. Are you married?
2. Tell me about your family.
3. What is your religion?

4. Where are you from?
5. May I call you _____ (first name)?
6. How much money do you make?
7. How much did you pay for your house/car?

Vocabulary

Sharing Personal Information

With a partner, share two examples for each of the following. Explain your answers. The boldface words are used by the speaker.

Something that . . .
- makes you feel **uncomfortable**
- makes you **frustrated**
- is **rewarding** to you
- needs **immediate** attention
- you've made a financial **investment** in

A person you . . .
- have a good **relationship** with
- **trust**
- know who has a lot of **patience**
- have had to **negotiate** with
- have had a long **friendship** with

Matching

Match the terms on the left with their definitions on the right.

_____ 1. contract   a. timeliness
_____ 2. developing   b. possibly
_____ 3. personal   c. establishing
_____ 4. potentially   d. formal agreement
_____ 5. process   e. organization
_____ 6. promptness   f. individual
_____ 7. structure   g. procedure

UNIT 4: Cross-Cultural Miscommunication   129

Filling in the Missing Words

Fill in the blanks with the most appropriate words.

| as well | confidence | enter into | turnaround time |
| business arena | details | sued | |

1. Joshua has so much _____ in himself that he believes he will never fail.
2. He will enter the _____ after being a teacher for many years.
3. Roberto's company will _____ an agreement with a new client.
4. I don't understand the contract. There are too many _____.
5. Ms. Garza was _____ for breaking the contract.
6. Sara enjoys hiking; she sometimes goes rock climbing _____.
7. Thanks to new technology and hard work, the company's _____ for production has been reduced by 30 percent.

Listening Comprehension Check

🎧 Listening for Information

Check the items that, according to the speaker, apply to each cultural group's approach to business.

1. *American Culture*
   - _____ a. Immediate
   - _____ b. Want everything now
   - _____ c. It's all about business, details, contract, and price
   - _____ d. Spend time with the negotiating partner
   - _____ e. Negotiate it now, sign on the dotted line, handshake, good-bye
   - _____ f. Frustrated abroad
   - _____ g. Suit and tie important
   - _____ h. Could be sued for asking about personal life

2. *Other Cultures*
   - _____ a. About relationships
   - _____ b. About making big money
   - _____ c. About developing confidence in each other
   - _____ d. About trust
   - _____ e. Slower process
   - _____ f. More rewarding process
   - _____ g. Requires persistence
   - _____ h. Investment in person and person's family

🎧 Listening for Ideas

Listen again and answer the questions. Discuss your answers with a partner.

1. What does the speaker mean by *sign on the dotted line*?
   _____
   _____

2. Circle the style of business relationship development the speaker prefers:

   United States   Other

   What does Ms. Skaggs say that gives you a clue of her preference?
   _____
   _____

3. According to the speaker, what is one reason why Americans are often frustrated?
   _____
   _____

4. What situation was the speaker referring to when she mentioned that an American might sue?
   _____
   _____

Discussion

Analyzing Situations and Discussing Quotations

Discuss the following.

1. Refer to the questions in the prelistening activity. When would it be acceptable to ask these questions in a business setting? Consider who you're talking to and how well you know the person.

2. Under what circumstances would you . . .
   - invite your boss to your house for dinner?
   - give gifts to your boss's kids?
   - give a gift to your teacher?
   - take a colleague out to lunch?

   Under what circumstances would taking any of the above actions be inappropriate?

3. *Time is money* is a popular saying in the United States. What does this mean? Do you agree? Why or why not? Based on what the speaker said, how do you think the expression *time is money* applies to Americans' attitudes toward business relationships?

4. *Americans are very friendly and very suspicious, that is what Americans are and that is what always upsets the foreigner, who deals with them, they are so friendly how can they be so suspicious; they are so suspicious, how can they be so friendly, but they just are.*—Gertrude Stein (1874–1946)

   What do you think this quotation means? How does it match your own experiences? Give an example.

Using Expressions

Business has many colorful idioms and expressions. The following expressions are commonly used in the business environment, but they are also used in other settings. Working in pairs, fill in the blanks. Then use context clues to help you guess the meanings.

break even	in the red
company man	signed on the dotted line
heads will roll	

1. After hours of negotiation, both parties agreed to the changes and _____.

2. Mr. Jones is a real _____; for thirty years he has always done what he felt was best for the company.

3. The company was _____ for many years before finally making a profit last year.

4. It usually takes a new business two or three years to _____.

5. I'm afraid that some _____ once our boss finds out how much money was wasted.

Further Study

Choose from the following.

1. Working with a partner, use the Internet to look for tips on how to develop business relationships in the United States and in one other country. Compare the similarities and differences. Report your findings to the class.

2. Research a multinational corporation (e.g., Microsoft, Toyota, Daimler-Chrysler, Samsung, Philips, Coca-Cola). Find out about the corporation's management style and investigate the reasons for its international success. Report your findings to the class.

3. Business professionals are becoming more aware of the need to enhance cultural sensitivity. As a result, they sometimes seek the assistance of consultants that specialize in cross-cultural training. Research a cross-cultural training company. Report on its programs and fees.

4. Search the Internet for five more business idioms or expressions. Write a sentence for each. Then using your sentences, teach these expressions to your classmates.

Web Activities

For additional activities related to this chapter, go to the *From College to Careers* website at **http://esl.college.hmco.com/students**.

UNIT 5

CONTROVERSIAL TOPICS

Skills Chart

Listening	Speaking	Vocabulary	Integrated Skills
■ Listening for • information • examples • ideas • definitions • missing words ■ Note-taking ■ Summarizing	■ Interviewing ■ Speaking off-the-cuff ■ Using scenarios to express opinions ■ Discussing a literary quotation ■ Expressing opinions ■ Discussing pros and cons	■ Guessing meaning from context ■ Categorizing ■ Identifying definitions ■ Filling in the missing words ■ Analyzing word connotations	■ Building consensus ■ Hypothesizing ■ Thinking critically ■ Making inferences ■ Creating a chart or concept map ■ Compiling and reporting data ■ Understanding irony and maxims ■ Making a presentation ■ Writing a paper

CHAPTER 22
Happy Death

John Hermann is a political science professor at a private university. He teaches constitutional law and judicial processes. His research primarily focuses on Supreme Court decision making.

Chapter Objectives

- Creating a concept map
- Categorizing
- Guessing meaning from context
- Identifying definitions
- Listening for definitions and examples
- Listening for missing words
- Understanding irony
- Discussing pros and cons
- Hypothesizing
- Using scenarios to express opinions
- Impromptu speaking
- Interviewing
- Creating a chart
- Making a presentation
- Writing a paper

Prelistening

Creating a Concept Map

Discuss the following with a partner.

1. Create a concept map to represent what you know or think about euthanasia. (See Chapter 11 for a brief explanation of concept maps.) Connect your ideas with lines or symbols to show their relationship to each other. Your map can be as simple or as elaborate as you choose. Then explain your concept map to another pair of students in your class.

   To help you get started, the following is a simple example of a concept map on the death penalty.

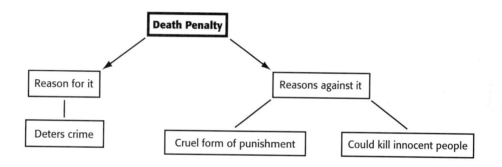

2. Why do you think euthanasia has become such a controversial issue in the United States?

Vocabulary

Categorizing

Work in pairs to categorize the following terms in the table. Then compare your choices with another pair of students and discuss any differences.

active euthanasia
branch of government
clear and convincing evidence
constitutional/constitution
illegal
invasive treatment
lethal dose of medication

no hope of recovery
nonelected branch
passive euthanasia
patient
quality of life
right to privacy
Supreme Court

terminally ill
terminate a life
up to the states
will
withholding treatment

Legal or Governmental Terms	Medical Terms

Guessing Meaning from Context

Replace the underlined word(s) in each sentence.

acknowledged	decisions	generous
as long as	dignity	issues
day in and day out	document	moreover

1. Here is an <u>important written paper</u> about your family history.
2. <u>If</u> my children do their homework, they can go to the movie.
3. Juanita is a great mother; <u>in addition</u>, she does a lot for the community.
4. Sasha has been building a house <u>continually</u> for almost a year now.
5. Jose is such a <u>giving</u> person that he donated 20 percent of his salary to charity.
6. Accepting a job offer and moving to another country were difficult <u>choices</u> to make.
7. Your friend finally <u>admitted</u> that he made a terrible mistake.
8. I am taking a few days off to deal with some <u>problems</u> at home.
9. Frank lost his job, but he didn't lose his <u>self-respect</u>.

Matching

Match the terms on the left with their definitions on the right.

_____ 1. controversial   a. cause to come about sooner than expected

_____ 2. fulfilling an objective   b. deeply personal or private in nature

_____ 3. hasten   c. different compared to something else

_____ 4. heritage   d. causing debate or disagreement

_____ 5. in contrast   e. tradition; custom
_____ 6. intimate   f. meddling
_____ 7. intrusive   g. caring
_____ 8. kind   h. completing a goal or purpose

Listening Comprehension Check

Listening for Definitions and Examples

Listen to the recording and answer the questions.

1. How does the speaker define the following terms?

    a. euthanasia
    _____
    _____

    b. passive euthanasia
    _____
    _____

    c. active euthanasia
    _____
    _____

2. According to the speaker, which type of euthanasia—passive or active—is more controversial?
   _____
   _____

3. Which type of euthanasia is constitutional as long as there is clear and convincing evidence of some sort?
   _____
   _____

4. Which are examples of rights that are *not* mentioned in the constitution?
    a. travel
    b. shaving
    c. medication
    d. abortion

5. Why does the speaker mention a dog?
_____
_____

Listening for Missing Words

Listen again and fill in the missing words.

The third and the trickiest issue is that, even though this is not mentioned in the (1) _____, there is a right to privacy in the United States, and the question is where does that right to privacy come from. It has been acknowledged that people have a right to travel. It's not mentioned in the (2) _____. They also have a right to shave or wear deodorant even though it's not mentioned in the (3) _____. It gets a little bit more (4) _____ when you're talking about issues of abortion, which the (5) _____ has included under privacy. But unlike abortion, (6) _____ is not considered part of our historical (7) _____, and, therefore, is not protected.

Understanding Irony

1. Read the following four statements. Cross out the statement that is NOT ironic.
    a. You stay up all night studying for a test but then fall asleep during the test.
    b. You run into a traffic jam after buying a new car.
    c. A police chief robs a bank.
    d. One of the world's richest people wins a ten million dollar lottery.

LANGUAGE NOTE:

Irony refers to an apparent contradiction between what might be expected and what actually is. Here are three examples:
- A cardiologist suffers a heart attack while giving a lecture on preventing heart attacks.
- A memory expert forgets what he is talking about.
- A famous person is scheduled to speak at a high school about the dangers of drinking. On the way to the school, he is arrested by the police for allegedly driving while drunk.

2. The speaker says, "Doctors take a Hippocratic oath. I like to call it a hypocritical oath, but it's a Hippocratic oath." What do you think he means? Some people would consider this to be an ironic statement. Do you agree?

Discussion

Discussing Pros and Cons

Discuss the following.

1. Discuss the pros and cons of euthanasia.

2. If you were terminally ill and your quality of life were deteriorating, would you want the option to choose euthanasia? Why or why not?

3. The speaker uses the example of a dog. Do you agree with the speaker's opinion that Americans are sometimes more humane to their pets than to family members? Explain.

4. Do you think euthanasia is a private decision? What should the government's role be? Explain.

5. The speaker discusses constitutional rights versus societal norms. What do you think he means? Which should take precedence? Why?

Scenarios: Expressing Opinions

Assume euthanasia is legal and you are the physician for the following patients. How would you handle each of the following cases? Discuss your opinion with a classmate who has a different point of view.

Case #1

Your patient is the head of a household who is experiencing excruciating pain from an incurable illness. He knows that the end will be slow and agonizing and will require expensive treatments that his insurance will not cover. To avoid suffering and putting his family in debt, he pleads with you to end his life.

Case #2

Your patient is an elderly woman who has terminal cancer. She is suffering a moderate amount of pain now, but she knows that it will get much worse in the next few months. She has always been an independent person and feels extremely depressed about her worsening state and her dependence on medical caregivers and relatives. She begs you to allow her to die with dignity.

Case #3

Your patient is a young man who contracted the HIV virus several years ago. He does not yet have full-blown AIDS but knows it is only a matter of time. He is suffering from both physical and emotional pain and does not see the point of continuing to deteriorate for months or even years. He believes that euthanasia is the most humane choice.

Case #4

Your seventy-year-old patient has been in a coma for five years, and tests show that there is no hope of recovery. The patient told her children ten years ago that if she were ever in a coma, she would not want to continue living.

Impromptu Speaking

John Hermann is extremely well organized when speaking off-the-cuff on a topic that is familiar to him. Although this kind of polished, spontaneous speaking ability can take many years to develop, practicing impromptu speaking is important for developing fluency in everyday interactions. Two ways of practicing this kind of speaking are expressing an opinion or talking about something that you are familiar with. Talk for one minute off-the-cuff on one of the following topics. A classmate will time you.

- Summarize the recording you just heard.
- Give your opinion on euthanasia.
- Give your opinion on the humane treatment of pets.

Further Study

Choose from the following.

1. Ask ten people if they are for or against legalizing active euthanasia. Then create a chart showing the results of the survey. Report your findings to the class.

2. Research physician-assisted suicide. Write a short paper or give a presentation to the class. Include the following:
   - What it is
   - How it is different from euthanasia
   - The state(s) in which it is legal

3. Research living wills and give a presentation on the topic to the class. Present the facts as well as your opinion.

4. Find out in which countries euthanasia is legal, when it was legalized, and the reasons for legalizing it. Report your findings to the class.

Web Activities

For additional activities related to this chapter, go to the *From College to Careers* website at **http://esl.college.hmco.com/students**.

CHAPTER 23
Prostitution in a Big City

Daneen Milam is a neuropsychologist who specializes in forensic psychology. In addition to providing counseling, Dr. Milam is frequently called to be an expert witness in capital murder trials. Here she tackles a highly controversial topic—prostitution.

Chapter Objectives

- Expressing opinions
- Building consensus
- Filling in the missing words
- Note-taking
- Summarizing
- Expressing opinions
- Analyzing word connotations
- Analyzing pros and cons
- Making a presentation
- Writing a paper

Prelistening

Expressing Opinions

Discuss the following.

1. What are the consequences of dropping out of high school?

2. What types of programs does the government provide for the poor?

3. *Prostitution is the world's oldest profession.* Discuss this statement with one of your classmates. Do you agree or disagree?

Think / Pair / Share

1. List three professions that you think are the most *dangerous*. Then share your list with a partner. Do you agree with each other? If not, create a new list of the three most dangerous professions by combining your ideas with those of your partner. You must reach a consensus. Then compare your new list with another pair of students in your class.

2. Repeat the process by listing three low-paying jobs. Why are these jobs so poorly paid? How can someone advance to higher paying jobs?

Vocabulary

Filling in the Missing Words

Fill in the blanks with the most appropriate words. Then listen to the recording and make any necessary changes.

Part I

food stamps
hang out
life span
minimum wage
shoplifting
street people
subsidized housing

1. Michael's _____ job makes it difficult for him to support his family.
2. The average _____ of an American male is almost eighty years.
3. Phil likes to _____ at his favorite nightclub; he's there almost every night.
4. The police charged the man with _____ for attempting to steal candy bars from the store.
5. The number of _____ has grown since the town's largest company went out of business.
6. The government provides _____ for some poor people to live in and _____ for groceries.

Part II

accessible
agency
alley
habit

limited
model (verb)
welfare

1. Now that Mr. Smith has a job, he no longer lives on _____.

2. Mary has a terrible cocaine _____ that costs her more than $100 a day.

3. It is dangerous to walk in a dark _____ in a high-crime area.

4. The amount of money you can make as a store clerk is _____.

5. The building is under renovation now and is not _____ to the public.

6. Roberta has become a fashion model. She works for a world-renowned _____ in New York. Next week she will _____ clothes for a fashion show in Paris.

Listening Comprehension Check

Note-Taking

The speaker is a psychologist in private practice who deals with some of the toughest cases of abuse and prostitution. Look at the following categories. Listen to the speaker and list the information that she mentions about each category. Some of the categories are detailed; others are global in scope and will require you to listen to the entire recording to get the information.

Ways the government helps the poor

_____
_____
_____

Types of low-paying jobs

_____
_____
_____

Ways women get into prostitution

_____
_____
_____

Types of drugs

_____
_____
_____

Ways to pay for a drug habit

_____
_____
_____

Why a street prostitute dies within two years

_____
_____
_____

Summarizing

Working in groups, discuss the notes you took in the previous exercise. Add or clarify any information that is not complete. Then use your notes to give an oral summary to the class.

Discussion

Expressing Opinions

Discuss the following.

1. How do you think the speaker is able to remain so positive and upbeat despite dealing with such tragic cases? Do you think that you would be able to emulate those qualities? Why or why not?

2. What role should the government play in helping the poor and homeless? Discuss your views on subsidized housing, food stamps, and other welfare programs.

3. Prostitution is legal in some places. Do you think that prostitution should be legal? Why or why not? If you think that prostitution should be legal, what are the implications for public health? If you think that prostitution should be illegal, who should be punished, and what should the penalties be?

4. Prostitution is a contributing factor to the global AIDS epidemic. What, if anything, should local governments do to regulate or control prostitution?

5. The speaker mentions that prostitution is a means of financing drug habits. The penalties for the possession of drugs vary from country to country and, in the United States, from state to state. How do you think legalizing drugs or lessening the penalties for the possession of drugs would impact prostitution? Should less hard-core drugs like marijuana be legalized? Why or why not?

Analyzing Word Connotations

LANGUAGE NOTE:

A dictionary provides the literal meaning, or denotation, of a word. However, to become fluent in another language, we must also learn the connotations of a word (i.e., a particular emotion or attitude that the word evokes in a native speaker). For example, the dictionary definition of both home and house is "a dwelling place." However, whereas house simply connotes a structure that one lives in, a home has many connotations (e.g., comfort—Home sweet home; security—My home is my castle).

Two or more words can frequently have the same meaning in English, but they often have quite different connotations. Some words sound softer, or more polite, than others; some words carry negative connotations; some come across as neutral. For example, the following three terms all have the same meaning: lied, misspoke, and stretched the truth. Can you guess which one is the softest sounding, which one is the most neutral, and which has the harshest sound? Softer, less direct terms are called euphemisms. Euphemism comes from the Greek word *euphemia*, meaning use of good words. We use euphemisms to avoid sounding strongly negative.

When you are uncertain about a word's connotation, pay careful attention to the context in which it is used. If you are still in doubt, ask a native speaker.

Each group of terms has the same meaning but different connotations. Use the scale to rate the connotation of each term: 1 = most polite (euphemism); 2 = neutral; 3 = least polite (most negative). If you're not sure, guess. Then compare your answers with those of a classmate.

Listen to the recording again and circle the words the speaker uses.

Term	Connotation Rating
disadvantaged	
economically deprived	
needy	
poor	
underprivileged	

Term	Connotation Rating
alcohol addiction	
chemical dependency	
drug addiction	
habit	
substance abuse	

Term	Connotation Rating
bums	
homeless	
street people	
vagrants	

Term	Connotation Rating
hooker	
lady of the night	
prostitute	
street walker	

Further Study

Choose one of the following topics to research. Then give a presentation or write a paper on the topic.

1. The pros and cons of one of the following:
   - legalized prostitution
   - legalized marijuana
   - legalized marijuana for medicinal purposes
2. Eligibility for food stamps in a state of your choice
3. Drug possession laws in two states

Web Activities

For additional activities related to this chapter, go to the *From College to Careers* website at **http://esl.college.hmco.com/students**.

CHAPTER 24 Water Rights

Dr. Charles Miller discusses water rights, an issue that is becoming more important in the United States and other parts of the world.

Chapter Objectives

- Discussing a literary quotation
- Identifying definitions
- Filling in the missing words
- Listening for ideas
- Listening for information
- Thinking critically
- Making inferences
- Understanding maxims
- Interviewing
- Compiling and reporting data
- Researching maxims
- Making a presentation

Prelistening

Discussing a Literary Quotation

Water, water everywhere, Ne [not] any drop to drink. This famous literary quotation comes from Samuel Taylor Coleridge's poem, *The Rhyme of the Ancient Mariner*. What do you think it means? What is the possible symbolism of water?

Vocabulary

Matching

Match the terms on the left with their definitions on the right.

_____ 1. access
_____ 2. bickering
_____ 3. conception
_____ 4. desperately
_____ 5. dinky
_____ 6. prior appropriation
_____ 7. reservoirs
_____ 8. sins
_____ 9. stream
_____ 10. treaty
_____ 11. tribes

a. a doctrine for prioritizing water rights based on the principle of "First in time, first in right."
b. small, unimportant
c. small river
d. urgently
e. arguing
f. American Indian nations
g. idea
h. written agreement
i. right of entry
j. lakes used to store water for community use
k. offenses

Filling in the Missing Words

Fill in the blanks with the most appropriate words.

appropriation   key
claim   priority
figured out   sue
flow   Supreme Court

1. Water is _____ to survival.
2. The big company refused to pay the farmer for water rights, so the farmer decided to _____.
3. You have to make water conservation a higher _____.
4. Los Angeles _____ how to address its water shortage problem.
5. Native American groups and the U.S. government have both laid _____ to water in the West.
6. The _____ of the river was interrupted by the new dam.
7. The _____ may have to rule on some water rights issues.
8. _____ refers to the right to use water for beneficial use.

> **LANGUAGE NOTE:**
>
> The speaker uses the expression *screw you*, which, in this context, means *I get what I need or deserve and I don't care what happens to you*. This expression is considered informal or vulgar.

Listening Comprehension Check

Listening for Ideas

The speaker discusses three issues related to water rights in the United States. Listen to the recording and answer the questions.

What does the speaker say about . . .

a. water usage in the West?

b. water usage in the East?

c. Native Americans' water rights?

Listening for Information

Which of the following did the speaker say? More than one answer may be correct.

a. Native Americans can claim prior appropriations.

b. The maxim "First in time, first in right" describes the water policy in the East and the West.

c. The Supreme Court's decisions regarding water rights has made previously inaccessible water accessible to Native Americans.

d. More creative ways to recycle water from the Colorado River are being developed.

e. Water was essential to Los Angeles' growth.

f. Water will become less and less of an important issue in the American West.

Discussion

Critical Thinking

Discuss the following.

1. Have you ever experienced a water shortage? If so, explain. What did the government do to help alleviate the shortage?

2. As the population grows in some dry or arid areas, water shortages are predicted. What responsibilities should individuals have, and what should the government do to help lessen the possibility of a shortage?

3. Look at the following map of the United States. What do you think Americans mean when they say East and West?

Maxims

Benjamin Franklin (1706–1790) was a renowned scientist, inventor, statesman, printer, musician, and economist. He was also a famous philosopher known for his maxims, some of which are listed here. Discuss the meaning of the following maxims with a partner.

1. Hunger never saw bad bread.
2. A man without a wife is but half a man.
3. Nothing but money is sweeter than honey.
4. One today is worth two tomorrows.
5. Speak little, do much.
6. Three may keep a secret if two of them are dead.

> **LANGUAGE AND CULTURAL NOTE**
>
> A wise saying is commonly referred to as a maxim. When discussing the idea of water rights in the West, the speaker brought up the maxim *First in time, first in right*. What does this mean? Do you think it is a wise approach? Why or why not?

Further Study

Choose from the following.

1. Find out where water in your city or community comes from and how it is monitored and replenished. Then prepare a report for the class.
2. Working in a group, each team member will ask five people the following question: *Which of the three issues do you think will become the most critical global problem in the next fifty years? Why?*
   - air pollution
   - oil shortage
   - water shortage

   Compile your group's data and present your findings to the class.
3. Find five more maxims and introduce them to the class.

Web Activities

For additional activities related to this chapter, go to the *From College to Careers* website at **http://esl.college.hmco.com/students**.

MORE OF THE REAL WORLD

Unit Outline

You may use the following chapters in lieu of or in addition to the chapters in Units 1–5:

- Unit 1/ Chapter A: Texts, Lies, and Final Exams
- Unit 2/ Chapter B: I'd Always Wanted to...
- Unit 3/ Chapter C: Permanent Materials Only
- Unit 4/ Chapter D: Doctors and Their Bedside Manners
- Unit 5/ Chapter E: E Pluribus Unum

CHAPTER A
Texts, Lies, and Final Exams

Dr. Charles Miller offers insights into higher education in the United States.

Chapter Objectives

- Sharing ideas
- Analyzing word families
- Guessing meaning from context
- Identifying definitions
- Note-taking
- Listening for details
- Expressing opinions and analyzing pros and cons
- Conducting research for a paper
- Writing a paper
- Interviewing
- Making a presentation

Prelistening

Sharing Ideas

Discuss the following.

1. Who have been your favorite teachers? Describe their teaching styles.
2. Do you prefer taking exams or writing papers? Explain.
3. What skills do you expect to learn at a university? How will these skills help you in your career or in your life?

Vocabulary

Analyzing Word Families

Fill in other forms of the words in the table. The words already in the chart are used by the speaker. Some words may not have a corresponding form for each category.

Noun	Verb	Adjective	Adverb
	analyze		
	assumes		
	contradict		
			critically
	engaging		
mission			
	persuades		
		strategic	
			ultimately

Guessing Meaning from Context

Replace the underlined word(s) in each sentence.

analyze   frankly   persuade
assume   give and take   proclaim
disparaging   mission   stuff

1. Did the salesman <u>influence</u> you to buy the car?
2. The president will <u>declare</u> Monday a national holiday.
3. Sam feels it is his <u>duty</u> to help the homeless.
4. My room is filled with all types of <u>things</u>.
5. I <u>suppose</u> that he will be home late tonight.
6. The detective should <u>examine</u> the information closely.
7. <u>Honestly</u>, I really don't care what he thinks.
8. There should be a <u>sharing of ideas</u> between teacher and student.
9. I was surprised that he had such <u>critical</u> remarks about the new house. I liked the house very much.

Identifying Definitions

Match the terms on the left with their definitions on the right.

_____ 1. contradict   a. confusing
_____ 2. critically   b. influence or stimulate someone to participate
_____ 3. draft (noun)   c. move
_____ 4. engage   d. an early version of a paper (not final product)
_____ 5. fundamentally   e. finally
_____ 6. obfuscating   f. basically
_____ 7. process   g. disagree with
_____ 8. transfer   h. procedure
_____ 9. ultimately   i. seriously; analytically

Listening Comprehension Check

Note-Taking

As you listen to the recording, fill in the table by writing the speaker's ideas about the following topics.

Topic	Speaker's Ideas
Teaching or taking morning classes	
Class lectures	
Critical thinking	
Textbooks and documents	
Writing	
Exams	

UNIT 6: More of the Real World   159

🎧 Listening for Details

Listen to the recording. Then change the following statements to make them true.

1. The speaker prefers teaching after lunch.
   _____
   _____
   _____

2. His mission in a morning class is to teach sleepy students whatever he can without getting too frustrated.
   _____
   _____
   _____

3. He doesn't try to engage students in class.
   _____
   _____
   _____

4. Students take American history thinking that they know nothing but find out that they actually know a lot.
   _____
   _____
   _____

5. According to the speaker, the approach to teaching American history in high school and college is almost identical.
   _____
   _____
   _____

6. The speaker believes that students can always depend on textbooks for accuracy.
   _____
   _____
   _____

7. He believes that texts rarely contradict each other.
   _____
   _____
   _____

8. His ambition is to have students write dates and facts.

   _____
   _____
   _____

9. He prefers exams to papers because exams are a stronger measure of a student's performance.

   _____
   _____
   _____

Discussion

Expressing Opinions and Analyzing Pros and Cons

Discuss the following.

1. The speaker enjoys teaching in the morning. Are you a morning person? Why or why not? If not, at what time of the day are you most productive? Explain.

2. The speaker described his teaching style as a constant give and take with the students (the Socratic method). What are the pros and cons of his teaching style? What teaching style do you prefer? Why?

3. Do you share the speaker's opinion that exams "don't teach anything"? Why or why not? Do you learn more from taking an exam or writing a paper? Explain.

4. Refer to the Note-Taking activity in Listening Comprehension Check. Write your opinions for each topic. Discuss your opinions with a classmate and compare your ideas with those of the speaker. How often do you agree/disagree? Explain.

Further Study

Choose from the following.

1. Find out who Socrates was and research the Socratic method. Write a short paper about the Socratic method. Compare and contrast this method to another one you are familiar with.
2. Ask two professors to describe their teaching style. Find out what skills they emphasize and what types of exams and research papers they assign. Present your findings to the class.

 ## Web Activities

For additional activities related to this chapter, go to the *From College to Careers* website at **http://esl.college.hmco.com/students.**

CHAPTER B

I'd Always Wanted to . . .

Dr. Daneen Milam talks about the road she took to become a psychologist.

Chapter Objectives

- Sharing expectations and goals
- Filling in the missing words
- Listening for chronological sequence, details, and past tense
- Expressing opinions and goals
- Impromptu speaking
- Interviewing
- Creating a chart
- Conducting research for a presentation
- Making a presentation
- Drawing conclusions
- Writing a paper in the past tense

Prelistening

Sharing Expectations and Goals

Discuss the following.

1. When you were a child, what did you think you would be when you grew up? How have your plans changed?
2. Why did you decide to go the college?
3. Why might someone wait until later in life to attend college?

Vocabulary

Filling in the Missing Words

Fill in the blanks with the most appropriate words.

Part I

ambition
dating
down there
evolved
golden times of my life

1. Her life has _____ from being a high school dropout to being a successful business owner.

2. Frank was _____ so many women that he could hardly find time to study.

3. Since high school, her _____ has been to get a law degree.

4. When I look back at the mid-1990s, I think of that period as one of those _____.

5. I grew up in Florida, but I have not been back _____ since moving to New York ten years ago.

Part II

grade point average (GPA)
junior college
keep up with
majoring
opportunity
scholarship
throw up

1. A _____ offers a two-year degree.

2. Getting a college degree can open up a great job _____.

3. Yuki's _____ improved because she studied much harder.

4. Tanya felt so nervous her first day of class that she thought she was going to _____.

5. My roommate is _____ in chemistry, and I'm studying economics.

6. Because I did not receive a _____, I must work part-time to pay for college.

7. The teacher spoke so fast, I couldn't _____ her.

Listening Comprehension Check

🎧 Listening for Chronological Sequence

The speaker organized her talk chronologically. Number the following statements to show the sequence of events in her life. The first one has been done for you.

_____ Got a bachelor's degree

_____ Studied freshman English at the age of thirty-two in a junior college

_____ Returned to the United States and was living in the Washington, D.C., area

_____ Attended Texas A&M University, thanks to a presidential scholarship

_____ Received her Master's degree

__1__ Married young and traveled

_____ Finished her two-year degree

_____ Was awarded a scholarship for women over the age of thirty

_____ Won a second scholarship to Trinity University

CULTURAL NOTE:

Someone who goes to college directly out of high school at the age of eighteen is usually referred to as a traditional student. People who attend college at an older age or while working and raising families are often referred to as nontraditional students. The number of nontraditional students has been increasing for several years now. Which type of student are you? Discuss the advantages and disadvantages of each type of student.

🎧 Listening for Details

Listen to the recording and answer the questions.

1. How old was the speaker when she went back to school?
   _____
   _____

2. What was she afraid of?
   _____
   _____

3. According to the speaker, what were the eighteen-year-olds majoring in?
   _____
   _____

4. What were the older students better at than the younger students?
   _____
   _____

5. What was her initial ambition?
   _____
   _____

Listening for Past Tense

The speaker uses past tense narration to tell the story of how she got her education. Listen again and write as many past tense verbs as you can.

_____   _____   _____
_____   _____   _____
_____   _____   _____
_____   _____   _____

Discussion

Expressing Opinions and Goals

Discuss the following.

1. What challenges do people face when attending college later in life? Give some examples. Are the challenges different for men and women? Explain.

2. What is the best way to balance education and family or personal demands?

3. Discuss your goals. What are your plans in five years? Ten years?

Impromptu Speaking

Impromptu speaking is important for developing fluency in everyday interactions. Expressing an opinion or talking about something that you are familiar with are two ways to practice this kind of speaking. Talk for one minute off-the-cuff on one of the following topics. A classmate will time you.

- The educational background of a family member
- Your career goals: Have they gone as you planned or have things just happened?
- What you wanted to be when you were growing up; compare with your current interests.

Further Study

Choose from the following.

1. With a partner, ask ten people what they think are the ideal ages to start college, get married, and have children. Make a chart of the results, and analyze your findings for the class.

2. Research the following information about your current educational institution:
   - the average age of the students
   - the most popular major
   - the number of traditional and nontraditional students

   What conclusions can you draw from the information you gathered? Present your findings to the class.

3. Do you know someone in your family who has chosen a nontraditional path to education? Write a short past tense narration describing that person's education and career goals.

4. Prepare a presentation about someone you admire (a famous person or family member) and describe that person's education and career choices.

Web Activities

For additional activities related to this chapter, go to the *From College to Careers* website at **http://esl.college.hmco.com/students.**

CHAPTER C
Permanent Materials Only

Listen to Dr. Heywood Sanders discuss one of his areas of expertise—urban development.

Chapter Objectives

- Sharing ideas
- Categorizing
- Making word associations
- Listening for details
- Note-taking
- Sharing ideas and supporting opinions
- Conducting research for a paper/presentation
- Writing a paper
- Interviewing
- Making a presentation
- Using a map to present information

Prelistening

Sharing Ideas

Discuss the following.

1. Have you ever lived in a large city? What was the ethnic makeup of that city?
2. What defines a neighborhood? Talk about a neighborhood in your city. Discuss the social or economic class and the ethnic makeup of that neighborhood.

3. What does discrimination mean? Why do people discriminate? What are some of the most common forms of discrimination?

4. What is the dictionary definition of a deed? (Hint: It is related to a legal document.) When do you think a person signs a deed? What do you think a deed restriction is?

Categorizing

Work with a partner to categorize the following terms. Then compare your categories with those of another pair of students in your class.

African American
Asian
clubhouse
color choice for home exterior limited
exercise room
gate access with security guard
Hispanic
houses made out of brick or stone
Italian
Jewish
jogging trail
Mexican
parks and playgrounds
paved driveways only
swimming pool
tennis courts
wooden fence only

Amenities	Deed Restrictions	Ethnic/Racial Group

Vocabulary

Making Word Associations

In each row, cross out the term that does not relate to the boldface word(s).

1. afford	have enough money	have the funds for	have energy
2. Anglo	Caucasian	black	white
3. assumed	took for granted	lived	supposed
4. assure	harm	promise	guarantee
5. better off	more money	less money	greater wealth
6. compass points	directions	bearings	investments
7. dramatic	uninspiring	spectacular	exciting
8. isolated	crowded	lonely	out-of-the-way
9. long haul	long period of time	considerable time	short run
10. prohibited	demonstrated	forbidden	illegal
11. radically	very	completely	superficially
12. restricted	limited	constrained	open
13. sector	part	reflection	area
14. secure	safe	vulnerable	protected
15. seemingly	apparently	outwardly	inwardly
16. sewer	drain	balcony	gutter
17. widely	narrowly	extensively	broadly

Listening Comprehension Check

Listening for Details

Listen to the recording and answer the questions.

1. Deed restrictions were used by home builders in the early twentieth century to do which of the following? Circle all that apply.

   a. assure home buyers that their homes were affordable

   b. protect and secure home buyers' investments

   c. secure the construction of the houses' foundations

   d. limit the ability of the purchaser to do certain things with one's land

2. What are examples of deed restrictions that the speaker mentions?

   a. had to use permanent materials

   b. couldn't sell to certain groups

   c. couldn't build fences

   d. had to have attached garages

3. Which racial groups were frequent victims of deed restrictions?

4. What public amenities were some neighborhoods missing?

Note-Taking

Listen again and write the key words that characterize the four regions of San Antonio. Then make a brief presentation to the class comparing the characteristics of each region.

North Side	South Side	West Side	East Side

Discussion

Sharing Ideas and Supporting Opinions

Discuss the following.

1. With a partner, brainstorm additional deed restrictions based on those you are familiar with or those that you think could exist.

2. As the speaker mentioned, deed restrictions at the turn of the twentieth century were used to keep so-called undesirable groups out of certain neighborhoods. Today, this kind of discrimination is illegal; however, other kinds of deed restrictions still exist, including having a percentage of a home built using brick, stucco, or other materials. These restrictions are viewed by some as a hidden form of discrimination used to keep people of a certain socioeconomic status out of neighborhoods. Others see

these restrictions as protecting a buyer's investment. Do you think that deed restrictions based on characteristics other than race are acceptable? Be specific and defend your position.

3. Describe the socioeconomic and ethnic or racial makeup of your childhood neighborhood or that of your parents. How has the neighborhood changed?

Further Study

Choose from the following.

1. Research the immigration patterns of an ethnic group in an American city (e.g., Chinese in San Francisco, Italians in New York, or Cubans in Miami). Include at least the periods (dates) of heavy immigration, shifts in economic status, and information on the formation of ethnic neighborhoods. Then present your findings to the class or write a short paper summarizing your data.

2. Interview two long-time residents in the city in which you are living. Ask them if their neighborhood's ethnic makeup has changed and, if so, in what way. Report your findings to the class.

3. Make a presentation to the class describing the characteristics of the city or neighborhood in which you live or grew up.

4. Research the development of one of the following:
   - Suburbs
   - Gated communities
   - High rises
   - Condominiums

   Find out when it became popular, why people moved there, and where it is commonly found. Then present your findings to the class.

5. Think about the speaker's description of San Antonio's neighborhoods. Use a map to show the location or boundaries of neighborhoods in your city. Are these areas based on race, ethnicity, religion, national origin, or social or economic status? What are they called? Present your information to the class.

 # Web Activities

For additional activities related to this chapter, go to the *From College to Careers* website at **http://esl.college.hmco.com/students.**

CHAPTER D: Doctors and Their Bedside Manners

Dr. Kimberly Bradley discusses the challenges some doctors have when relating to their patients.

Chapter Objectives

- Supporting opinions and formulating questions
- Guessing meaning from context
- Filling in the missing words
- Using homonyms
- Listening for information
- Agreeing or disagreeing
- Conducting research for a paper/presentation
- Writing a paper
- Interviewing
- Making a presentation

Prelistening

Supporting Opinions and Formulating Questions

Discuss the following.

1. What do you look for in a doctor? What should characterize the doctor-patient relationship? Why? Look at the list and check whether you think each quality is important or unimportant for a doctor to have. Discuss your choices with a classmate.

Quality	Important	Not Important	Quality	Important	Not Important
communicative			humorous		
compassionate			knowledgeable		
conservative			matter-of-fact		
curious			open-minded		
determined			polite		
direct			persistent		
educated			reserved		
formal			serious		
friendly			trustworthy		
helpful			understanding		

2. As a new parent, you are looking for a pediatrician for your child. Write five questions that you want to ask a prospective pediatrician to help you select the one that best meets your needs and expectations. Share your questions with a classmate.

Vocabulary

Guessing Meaning from Context

Replace the underlined word in each sentence.

concept   requires
fussy   route/track
rather

1. I didn't follow a traditional <u>path</u> to medical school because I wanted to travel after I graduated from college.

2. Medical school <u>necessitates</u> serious focus and studying.

3. It's 8:00 already. You're <u>quite</u> late.

4. That's a brilliant idea you have—what a <u>thought</u>.

5. Stuart's son is a <u>selective</u> eater. He likes only pizza, hot dogs, and sweets.

Filling in the Missing Words

Fill in the blanks with the most appropriate words.

Part I

boards
humanistic approach
just do it
life experiences
offering
osteopathic training
what I was looking for

1. For its tenth anniversary, the clinic is _____ a free diabetes screening.

2. _____ combines traditional medicine and manipulation.

3. To become a physician, you must pass the _____.

4. Osteopathy offers a(n) _____ to medicine.

5. The university had exactly _____.

6. Having lived in so many countries has given her wonderful _____.

7. After a while, you have to stop complaining and _____.

Part II

challenging
difficulty
doc
interviewing
juggling
MDs
programs
relating to
share

1. Many of the courses I took at Harvard University were _____.

2. In a(n) _____ class in medical school, students learn how to better communicate with their patients.

3. Dr. Jones has trouble _____ the fact that her patient is struggling to pay the bills.

4. Martha has _____ attending medical school, taking care of a baby, helping her mother, and living on a low income. That's a lot of _____ to do.

5. Children need to learn to _____ toys with their friends.

6. _____ is an informal abbreviation for doctor.

7. Osteopaths and _____ take the same boards.

8. Good universities have many different _____ for their students.

Using Homonyms

Homonyms are words that are pronounced the same but have a different meaning and spelling (e.g., *pair* and *pear*; *they're*, *there*, and *their*). First fill in the blanks with the correct homonyms. Then listen to the recording and circle the word in each pair that the speaker uses.

1. one/won
   a. He is the right _____ for the job.
   b. He _____ the game, but it wasn't easy.

2. patience/patients
   a. It takes a lot of _____ to be a doctor.
   b. A popular doctor will see a lot of _____.

3. dual/duel
   a. Rick holds _____ citizenship; he is a citizen of two different countries.
   b. In the old days, men would settle their differences by having a _____.

4. buy/by
   a. Come _____ the mall.
   b. I'll _____ you lunch.

5. loan/lone
   a. Jack took out a _____ to help pay for his child's college education.
   b. Mr. Thompson is the _____ survivor of the plane crash.

FROM COLLEGE TO CAREERS: Doctors and Their Bedside Manners

Listening Comprehension Check

Listening for Information

Listen to the recording and answer the questions.

1. Which of the following are true according to the speaker?
   a. Osteopathic training is challenging because it is academically similar to a medical doctor's training.
   b. In Texas, MDs and osteopaths take different boards.
   c. Being an osteopath requires you to relate to people differently than MDs do.
   d. Many MD programs are starting to take a more humanistic approach.

2. Which of the following is the traditional education route mentioned by the speaker?
   a. internship → college → med school
   b. high school → college → med school
   c. work experience → high school → med school

3. What two examples does she give of how traditional track students could not relate to the life demands of ordinary people?
   _____
   _____

4. Why does she say, "Are you going to loan me some money, doc?"
   _____
   _____

Discussion

Expressing Agreement or Disagreement

Decide how closely the statements reflect your opinion. On the line next to each statement, write A if you agree, N if you neither agree nor disagree, or D if you disagree. Then discuss your answers with a classmate.

_____ 1. Doctors are trustworthy.

_____ 2. It is important to have good rapport with your physician.

_____ 3. Doctors are infallible.

_____ 4. It is essential to get a second opinion for any major diagnosis.

_____ 5. Doctors are primarily concerned with money and prestige.

_____ 6. Eye contact with a doctor is important.

_____ 7. Female doctors are more compassionate than male doctors.

_____ 8. Overall, doctors care most about improving the lives of their patients.

_____ 9. Doctors should establish trust with their patients by encouraging them to ask questions.

_____ 10. The Western approach to medicine is the most scientific approach.

_____ 11. Doctors should avoid medical jargon when speaking to patients.

_____ 12. Doctors should be reminded that it is the patients who pay their salaries.

_____ 13. Doctors do not need to explain everything to patients because it may lead to confusion and anxiety.

_____ 14. An important way for a physician to create a relaxed environment is to call patients by their first names.

_____ 15. If you don't understand what your doctor is saying, then you should ask a lot of questions until you do.

_____ 16. If a doctor does not answer your questions satisfactorily, consider finding another doctor.

_____ 17. The appearance and comfort of the waiting area in a doctor's office reflects the doctor's attitude toward patients.

_____ 18. A doctor needs to recognize that time is valuable to patients by not keeping them waiting too long.

_____ 19. A doctor should try to understand a patient's lifestyle and family situation to better understand the needs of the whole person.

_____ 20. Due to doctors' extensive education, patients can be assured that they are reliable sources of health information.

Further Study

Choose from the following.

1. Research one of the following types of alternative approaches to medicine and write a brief description. Include the reasons you would or would not want to use this approach.

   - acupressure
   - acupuncture
   - chiropractic
   - herbalism
   - homeopathy
   - massage therapy
   - naturopathy
   - osteopathy
   - reflexology

2. Ask two people who have used a holistic medical practitioner to talk about their experiences. Report what you learned from these interviews to the class.

3. Ask three people what qualities they look for in a doctor. Find out why these qualities are important to them. Report your findings to the class.

Web Activities

For additional activities related to this chapter, go to the *From College to Careers* website at **http://esl.college.hmco.com/students.**

CHAPTER E
E Pluribus Unum

Dr. Felecia Briscoe discusses a topic that has been important to many Americans since the founding of our country—state and local control versus federal control. In this instance, she's discussing the pros and cons of local and federal control of education.

Chapter Objectives

- Building consensus
- Analyzing word families
- Listening for missing words
- Note-taking
- Expressing opinions
- Using *if* clauses
- Conducting research for a report/presentation
- Writing a report
- Interviewing
- Making a presentation

Prelistening

Think / Pair / Share

Pick the five items that you think are most important for a well-rounded education. Then share your list with a partner. Do you agree with each other? If not, create a new list with your partner by combining your ideas. You must reach a consensus. Next compare your new list with another pair of students in your class.

adequate funding
extracurricular activities
innovative teaching techniques
modern facilities
parent involvement
standardized testing
strict discipline

strong government supervision
student motivation
teacher education
teacher experience
teacher salaries
varied curriculum
well-trained administrators

Vocabulary

Analyzing Word Families

Fill in other forms of the words in the table. The words already in the chart are used by the speaker. Some words may not have a corresponding form for each category.

Noun	Verb	Adjective	Adverb
approach; approaches			
	characterizing		
control			
difference		different	
equity			
individuals			
		local; localized	
		matriarchal	
		patriarchal	

Listening Comprehension Check

Listening for Missing Words

Listen to the speaker discuss centralized versus localized control of public education in the United States. Then fill in the missing words. Some words will be used more than once.

Using grammatical clues may help you, although you will note that not all of the excerpts are grammatically correct. Also, the speaker uses different word forms (e.g., diverse, diversity, diversified), so listen for the forms she uses. This reflects the way people really talk.

approach/approaches
centralized
control
difference/different
diversity/diversified/diverse
entrenched
equity

individuals
local/localized
matriarchal
patriarchal
product
standardized
uniformity

1. Schools should be far more _____ than they are.

2. Schools in Las Vegas are not that _____ than schools in Maine or schools in Florida.

3. They're pretty much churning out what you might call the mass-produced _____ of students.

4. Partly it's in the name of _____. If I'm being educated in Alaska, I should be able to go to New York City and fit right in.

5. If all the curriculums are the same, they are being taught to the same _____ tests, we are getting everybody that's thinking the same way.

6. There are no _____ of ideas.

7. We've had some pretty _____ problems in our society that don't seem to be going away.

8. If we want to begin to solve things in our society, we need a _____ of _____.

9. I think it would be better if we had more localized _____ over education.

10. Some people say the way of characterizing the difference between this is local control or _____ control is to say that most people don't know what they're doing—the masses.

11. And so it's best if you have a _____ or _____ figures that know what's best for people, and this tells them what to do.

12. And the other people say, no, no, this would be the Thomas Jefferson _____, you know, that the masses are really _____, rational folks who can in fact figure out what's best for them.

13. So, if we give people _____ control, then you're basically saying the people can figure out what's best for them.

14. I think with _____ control, you're going to get a lot more _____.

15. I think it's pretty frightening to me the degree of _____ in schools and students throughout the United States.

LANGUAGE NOTE:

Americans have different expressions for addressing two or more people. *You all*, sometimes pronounced *y'all*, is popular in the south; *you guys* and *youse guys* tend to be used in the Northeast. *Youse* is also heard in the Northeast, especially in large cities such as New York and Boston and is also common in Irish English. *You-uns*, which is heard in western Pennsylvania and the Appalachians, probably comes from the Scotch-Irish roots of many Europeans who settled in these areas.

Note-Taking

1. The speaker presents two sides of the debate on localized versus centralized control of education. In the table list the arguments that the speaker makes.

Localized Control of Education	Centralized Control of Education

2. Which type of control does the speaker prefer? Why?

CULTURAL NOTE:

Public versus *private schools* (kindergarten to twelfth grade)

Public schools are open to all residents who live in a particular area. Anyone can attend, and there is no tuition. Public schools are funded by local, state, and federal governments, of which property taxes constitute a major source of the funding. Each state establishes its own academic standards.

Private schools, on the other hand, charge tuition, which can be expensive. They can also have a selective admissions policy. Some private schools cater to a particular clientele (e.g., an all-boys military school, a college preparatory school, or a religious school).

Discussion

Expressing Opinions

Discuss the following.

1. The speaker expresses her opinion in the opening statement: "Schools should be far more diversified than they are." She then presents both sides of the argument before giving her opinion again. What phrases does the speaker use to indicate that she is expressing her opinion?

2. Here are some ways to express your opinion. Can you think of any others? Use these expressions in your responses to the following questions.

    From my perspective . . .

    I believe . . .

    I think . . .

    I lean toward . . .

    I tend to go with . . .

    I feel . . .

    In my opinion . . .

    In my point of view . . .

    In my view . . .

    My belief is . . .

    a. How much control should the national government have over local educational matters? Are you in favor of standardized testing for the whole country? Explain.
    b. What do you think about the idea of educational equity? Diversity?
    c. Do you agree or disagree with the speaker's ideas on education? Explain.
    d. If money were no object, would you choose public or private schools for your child (children)? Explain.
    e. How much responsibility do teachers have for the success or failure of their students? Explain.

Using If Clauses: Hypothetical or Possibility

This speaker uses *if* clauses to introduce possible arguments that people on both sides of the debate might use. Speaking hypothetically is useful for introducing various perspectives in a somewhat neutral way; it allows your audience to remain open when you introduce your point of view. The following statements are from the recording you just heard. Listen again and note these and other examples.

- If I'm being educated in Alaska, I should be able to go to New York City and fit right in.
- But if all the curriculums are the same, they are being taught to the same standardized tests.
- If we want to begin to solve things in our society, we need a diversity of approaches.
- If you don't deny them information, everybody can figure it out.

Complete the *if* clauses below.

1. If I inherit a million dollars,

2. If I am living in Hawaii,

3. If your friend wants to learn English,

4. If you want to take a vacation,

5. If we try to solve the world's problems,

Further Study

Choose from the following.

1. Research the public school system or district from a city you are familiar with or interested in learning about. Write a short report describing its structure, funding sources, use of standardized tests, and other factors.

2. Prepare a short presentation expressing your opinion on the importance of diversity and/or equity in education.

3. Research the Supreme Court decision *Brown v. Board of Education*. Write a short report discussing its importance in American education.

4. Ask five people if they attended public or private schools from kindergarten through the twelfth grade. Also ask them about the quality of their education. Report your findings to the class.

5. Thomas Jefferson was one the founding fathers of the United States. Research one of his contributions and tell the class about it.

Web Activities

For additional activities related to this chapter, go to the *From College to Careers* website at **http://esl.college.hmco.com/students.**

APPENDIX

Unit 1: Chapter 5:
When I Finish College, I Want to Be . . .

Discussion

Twenty Questions

List A

air traffic controller
diplomat
firefighter
international businessperson
lawyer
magician
mechanic
musician
president
race car driver
secretary
tour guide
veterinarian

List B

actor
archaeologist
astronaut
ballerina
chef
computer scientist
mail carrier
nuclear engineer
professional golfer
salesperson
teacher
television news reporter
writer

Unit 3: Chapter 13:
Never Assume Anything

Prelistening

Challenging Your Assumptions

1. 116 years (1337 to 1453)
2. Ecuador
3. Sheep, hogs, and horses
4. Squirrel fur
5. Crimson
6. New Zealand; they are also known as kiwi fruit.
7. Orange
8. Pink
9. North America; they are a member of the sunflower family.
10. Dogs; the Latin name was *Insularia canaria*: Island of the Dogs.

Discussion
Completing Quotes

1. We are entitled to make almost any reasonable assumption but should resist making conclusions until evidence requires that we do so.—Steve Allen
2. Never assume, for it makes an ASS out of U and ME.—Unknown
3. Most of our assumptions have outlived their uselessness.—Marshall McLuhan
4. If we all worked on the assumption that what is accepted as true is really true, there would be little hope of advancement.—Orville Wright

Unit 4: Chapter 18: The Spirit of African Hospitality

Prelistening
Africa Quiz

1. The Republic of Sudan, which is 967,500 square miles (2,505,816 square kilometers)
2. Gambia, which is 4,353, square miles (11,300 square kilometers)
3. Cairo
4. Christianity and Islam
5. 800–1,000
6. Nigeria
7. The Nile, which is 4,241 miles (6,825 kilometers) long
8. The largest (nonpolar) desert in the world is the Sahara, in north Africa, which spans an area approximately 3.5 million square miles (9 million square kilometers). It stretches into eleven countries.
9. Ethiopia
10. Between 1000 and 2000 (85 percent of Africans speak fifteen core languages)